BONHOMME RICHARD
VS
SERAPIS

Flamborough Head 1779

MARK LARDAS

First published in Great Britain in 2012 by Osprey Publishing,
Midland House, West Way, Botley, Oxford, OX2 0PH, UK
44-02 23rd Street, Suite 219, Long Island City, NY 11101, USA

E-mail: info@ospreypublishing.com

OSPREY PUBLISHING IS PART OF THE OSPREY GROUP

A CIP catalog record for this book is available from the British
Library

Print ISBN: 978 1 84908 785 8
PDF ebook ISBN: 978 1 84908 786 5
ePub ebook ISBN: 978 1 78096 448 5

Page layout by: Ken Vail Graphic Design, Cambridge, UK
Index by Judy Oliver
Typeset in ITC Conduit and Adobe Garamond
Maps by bounford.com
Originated by PDQ Media, Bungay, UK
Printed in China through Bookbuilders

12 13 14 15 16   10 9 8 7 6 5 4 3 2 1

Osprey Publishing is supporting the Woodland Trust, the UK's
leading woodland conservation charity, by funding the dedication
of trees.

www.ospreypublishing.com

Author's acknowledgments

Thanks go to the Houston Maritime Museum and its dedicated staff. University of
Houston-Clear Lake's Neumann Library was an invaluable source of material on
this book and many others that I have done over the years. I also need to thank
Bruce Biskup, a co-worker when we both worked at Boeing, Houston and a fellow
naval history enthusiast and my friends at the Gulf Coast Historic Ship Model
Society.

Author's note

The following abbreviations indicate the sources of the illustrations used in this
volume:

AC – Author's collection

AC-HMM – Author's collection, photo taken in the Houston Maritime Museum

BOOS – *Book of Old Ships*, Dover Publishing

LoC – Library of Congress, Washington, DC

MOA-UM – Making of America, University of Michigan

NHHF – United States Navy History and Heritage Command, Washington, DC

USN – United States Navy

Other sources are listed in full

Author's dedication

This book is dedicated to John Kendall and Ben Pfeiffer of the Houston Maritime
Museum. Their enthusiasm for maritime history is an example to everyone who
knows them.

Artist's note

Readers may care to note that the original paintings from which the battlescene,
quarterdeck views, and cover art were prepared are available for private sale. All
reproduction copyright whatsoever is retained by the Publishers. All enquiries
should be addressed to:

Giuseppe Rava
Via Borgotto 17
48018 Faenza (RA)
Italy
info@g-rava.it
www.g-rava.it

The Publishers regret that they can enter into no correspondence upon this matter.

Editor's note

Since the United States used British weights and lengths during the American
Revolutionary Wars, UK imperial measurements (e.g. long tons) are used
throughout this book. The following data will help in converting between US
customary, imperial, and metric measurements:

1 nautical mile (UK) = 1.853km

1yd = 0.9m

1ft = 0.3m

1in = 2.54cm/25.4mm

1 long ton = 1.016 metric tons

1 long ton = 1.12 short tons

1lb = 0.45kg

CONTENTS

INTRODUCTION

The captain of the British 44-gun ship *Serapis* had entered the battle confident of ultimate victory. Richard Pearson had only two ships to protect the convoy under his charge, his own *Serapis* and the smaller 20-gun sloop-of-war *Countess of Scarborough*, armed with 6-pounder long guns. Pearson counted six warships in the enemy's squadron, including a pair of frigates, three minor vessels, and another two-deck warship that seemed roughly the size of his own command. Yet Pearson felt that the odds were not nearly as bad as the raw numbers indicated. He was, he believed, fighting a group of privateers, commissioned by the rebel Colonials.

For privateers there was no profit in fighting warships, like his. Privateering was a legalized form of piracy, with the main objective of capturing enemy merchantmen. At first Pearson thought his main task would be to keep his two warships between the privateers and the convoy long enough to allow the merchant ships he was escorting to escape. He was not surprised when two of the privateers engaged the escorts. The smaller of the two frigates went for *Countess of Scarborough* and the big two-decker paired off against *Serapis*. That was a standard tactic – tying up the escorting warships allowed the unengaged privateers to chase the merchantmen. What surprised him was that the two-decker pressed its attack against *Serapis*.

It was not unwelcome, however. Although the two ships appeared evenly matched, Pearson valued the opportunity presented. A victory could make his name. *Serapis* was a new ship, with a well-drilled crew. After exchanging a few broadsides it became apparent that the Continental ship was less formidable that it appeared. Its broadsides were ragged, and the rate of fire slower than his own. Furthermore, after firing twice, the enemy's lower-deck guns had fallen silent.

Pearson recognized that the enemy was full of spirit, regardless. The Continentals had already once attempted to board *Serapis*. Now, however, Pearson had placed *Serapis*

across the bow of the enemy ship. While *Serapis* was at an angle where it could not yet fire on the Continental ship, Pearson felt that he could turn his ship to bear his guns. Confidently, Pearson called to his opponent, shouting "Has your ship struck?"

His opposite number, a short man with a pugnacious temper, immediately replied, "I have not yet begun to fight." Nor had he. The fight would continue for another four hours. Along with the Continental captain's defiant response, the battle would become so famous as to become legend as well as history. The battle of Flamborough Head became the most famous naval action of the American Revolutionary Wars. Larger and more decisive actions – Ushant, the battle of the Chesapeake, The Saintes – would become almost forgotten historical footnotes, of interest only to historians and naval buffs. But the battle of Flamborough Head became a symbol for both the United States and Great Britain.

For the United States, the battle became a symbol of all that was American – resolution, determination, and a willingness to press on to victory even when the odds were against you. John Paul Jones, who commanded the two-deck warship *Bonhomme Richard* during the battle, became the standard by which all subsequent United States Navy officers would measure themselves.

For the British, the battle symbolized the Royal Navy's tenacity and dedication to duty. Richard Pearson was forced to strike his colors, but he did so only after

The battle of Flamborough Head at its climax. To the left is the match between *Pallas* and *Countess of Scarborough*. To the right can be seen *Bonhomme Richard* locked into *Serapis*, with *Alliance* watching. This painting shows the ships much closer than they actually were. (NHHC)

protecting the convoy under his charge, and only after a second Continental warship came to the aid of *Bonhomme Richard* – Pearson did not know the second Continental ship threatened his opponent as well as his own ship.

While large fleet actions such as Trafalgar often decided the naval phase of the wars of which they were part, single-ship actions – such as the one fought between *Bonhomme Richard* and *Serapis* – were often equally famous. The War of 1812 duel fought between USS *Constitution* and HMS *Guerrière* achieved fame, as did the action between HMS *Nymphe* and the French frigate *La Cléopâtre* at the beginning of the French Revolutionary Wars. Duels between ships-of-the-line occasionally occurred, such as the brawl between HMS *Mars* and *Hercule* in 1798. A year before the battle of Flamborough Head an action between the frigates HMS *Arethusa* and the French *Belle Poule* became so famous that it inspired a ladies' hairstyle, the Belle Poule, which featured a model ship as a hat.

Those battles featured ships-of-the-line or frigates. Both represented a sailing navy's "first team." A ship-of-the-line was a navy's main weapon – heavy warships intended to mete out and absorb punishment. The frigate was its primary scout, a warship intended to seek out enemy fleets and duel with its counterparts. Both were expected to fill the starring role represented by participation in a ship-to-ship duel.

Neither *Bonhomme Richard* nor *Serapis* was a ship-of-the-line or a frigate – despite frequent claims that they were frigates. Rather, both belonged to an anomalous class of warship known as two-deckers. Like many ships-of-the-line they possessed two full gun decks, with additional guns mounted on their forecastle and quarterdeck. They

Britain felt their sailors to be superior to those of all other nations. As shown in this 1780 cartoon, Jack Tar was thought capable of besting four foreign sailors. (LoC)

were a type of miniature ship-of-the-line. But two-deckers were considered too small to stand in a line-of-battle. Their scantlings were too light to absorb the punishment meted out by a ship-of-the-line, and their guns too light to create the damage that a broadside of a ship-of-the-line created. Nor were two-deckers as fast or weatherly as frigates. They were slower. Even modest seas could prevent a two-decker from using its lower gun deck.

Two-deckers were a navy's reserve team, not intended as ship-killers. They were auxiliaries – convoy escorts, flagships in remote stations that were unworthy of a ship-of-the-line but too important for just a frigate, and cargo-carriers in waters requiring a heavily armed ship. The ultimate irony of the battle of Flamborough Head is that a battle that has become a symbol of naval combativeness was fought by two ships never intended to fight ship-to-ship duels.

CHRONOLOGY

1731
March — Richard Pearson born.

1745
— Richard Pearson joins Royal Navy as a volunteer.

1747
July 6 — John Paul Jones born.

1765
November 28 — *Duc de Duras* launched.

1775
April 19 — American Revolutionary Wars begin with the battles of Lexington and Concord.
October 13 — Continental Navy is established when the Continental Congress authorizes purchase of two warships.
December 7 — John Paul Jones receives a commission as a lieutenant in the Continental Navy.

1776
May 10 — John Paul Jones takes command of sloop-of-war *Providence*.
May 10 — John Paul Jones given command of sloop-of-war *Alfred*.

1777
February 21 — John Paul Jones promoted to captain.
June 14 — John Paul Jones takes command of sloop-of-war *Ranger*.

1778
February 14 — *Ranger* is saluted by the French Navy, marking the first time the American flag is recognized by a sovereign nation.
April 24 — USS *Ranger* captures HMS *Drake* off Carrickfergus, Ireland.

Shortly after the alliance between France and the United States was concluded, France recognized the United States as an independent nation when the French Navy formally saluted the Continental sloop-of-war *Ranger* in Quiberon Bay on February 14, 1778. (LoC)

The naval power of the new United States lay mainly in small warships, especially privateers, which would capture British merchant vessels and harry British warships. (USN)

1779

February 4	John Paul Jones given command of *Duc du Duras*, which is renamed *Bonhomme Richard*.
March 4	HMS *Serapis* launched.
August 14	Accompanied by privateers *Monsieur* and *Granville*, and commanding a squadron consisting of *Bonhomme Richard*, *Alliance*, *Pallas*, *Vengeance*, and *Cerf*, Jones sails from Île de Groix roadstead.
September 2	Battle of Flamborough Head.
October 2	Jones's squadron arrives at Texel, in the Netherlands.
November 12	*Serapis* turned over to the French Navy.

1781

July	As a French warship, *Serapis* burns and sinks off Madagascar.

1788

April 15	John Paul Jones goes to Russia and takes an admiral's commission in the Russian Navy.
June 28–29	John Paul Jones commands the inshore squadron at the 2nd battle of Limons in the Black Sea.

1792

July 18	John Paul Jones dies in Paris.

1800

	Richard Pearson is appointed lieutenant-general of Greenwich Hospital.

1806

January 26	Richard Pearson dies.

DESIGN AND DEVELOPMENT

18TH-CENTURY NAVAL ARCHITECTURE

By 1700, the design of the standard major oceangoing warship had evolved into the configuration it would maintain for the next 100 years. It was a configuration that we associate with the wooden sailing ship even today – three square-rigged masts and two or more full tiers of guns running the length of the ship.

This configuration was then used by all ships large enough to be commanded by an officer holding the rank of captain in the Royal Navy or its equivalent rank in other navies – ships that were known as either frigates, two-deckers, and ships-of-the-line. In 1700 the true frigate did yet not exist, only emerging in the middle of the 18th century. The cruiser and escort roles were instead filled by ships mounting two complete gun decks; albeit smaller vessels than ships-of-the-line, the name given to warships deemed worthy of joining the line-of-battle in which naval actions were then fought. Two-deckers were simply smaller versions of the ship-of-the-line. Where ships-of-the-line mounted at least 64 guns, two-deckers split as few as 30 or as many as 60 guns between two gun decks.

One reason for this was that the hulls of virtually all seagoing ships had the same basic shape. The length of the ship at the waterline was 3.6 to 3.8 times greater than the breadth of the ship. A ship's draft was typically one-seventh to one-eighth of its length at the waterline. Some ships were larger and others were smaller, but all shared this ratio for their principal dimensions. The two-decker was an outgrowth of these dimensions, and wooden construction.

In part, ship design was limited by the innate conservatism of mariners and naval architects. Since Europeans did not cross oceans before 1500, transoceanic ships were still relatively new. Prior to that ships were intended to spend only days, not weeks or months, at sea. Longer voyages meant bigger ships, and shipwrights soon learned that the old designs worked poorly and scaled up badly. The three-masted warship that emerged by 1700 emerged from trial-and-error experimentation and the lessons of often-fatal experience. What worked was more important than what might be best. One result of this conservatism was the standard use of transverse-framed hulls, made almost exclusively of wood. Even most fastenings were wooden pegs called treenails.

The ratio used for the hull dimensions was the consequence of wood's structural limitations. Narrower ships tended to break apart due to wave action working over the length of the ship. Wider ships moved too slowly and were hard to steer. Similarly, a ship's draft was dictated by its length. A ship much shallower than one-eighth of its length could be pushed excessively sideways rather than driven forward by the wind, rendering it uncontrollable in gales. A ship much deeper than one-seventh of its length was limited in terms of the ports at which it could call. The properties of wood also limited ships' length to less than 180ft at the waterline as hulls longer than this flexed or "worked" too much at sea.

Hulls had bluff bows, full hulls forward, and a narrow, deep stern. Naval architects called the hull form "cod's head and mackerel tail." It was not the most efficient hull form. Naval architecture was emerging as a true engineering field by 1700, but the principles were then less the result of engineering analysis than of precedent and rule of thumb. In the 19th century, naval architects learned that ships sailed faster with a fine bow and a full stern. But "cod's head and mackerel tail" yielded a ship that survived rough seas, while carrying a large cargo for the hull dimensions.

To a casual observer a two-deck ship seemed to have between four and seven decks, but many of these were only partial decks. At the lowest level, just above the keel and frames forming the bottom of the ship, was the hold. Food, water, cargo stowed in barrels, and ballast was carried at this level. Ballast was either shingle – fist-sized rocks – or iron bars and "pigs" (ingots). Additionally, the anchor cable was stowed in the hold, forward in a section called the cable tier.

On a warship, above the hold, was a series of platforms called the orlop. While sometimes called a "deck" these platforms were often discontinuous, and frequently at different levels. These were used for goods that should not be stored in the hold, such as spare sails, carpenter's timber and equipment, bosun's stores, bread, and

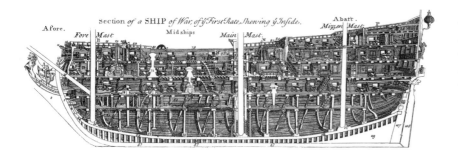

This cross-section of a first-rate ship-of-the-line shows the basic internal arrangement of a sailing-era warship. From the keel up: the hold, orlop, lower gun deck, middle gun deck, upper gun deck, forecastle and quarterdeck, and poop. (AC)

Whether the ship was a small warship, like USS *Lexington* shown here, or a three-deck ship-of-the-line, the hull dimensions had roughly the same ratio of length to breadth to draft. (NHHC)

surgeon's stores. It was the location of the surgery during battle – in the cockpit, amidships. Additionally junior warrant officers, such as midshipmen, and various mates were occasionally lodged there. Merchantmen, with smaller crews and wanting the largest possible hold volume for cargo, often did not install orlops.

Above the orlop was the lower deck, the lowest full deck on a ship, which typically ran 4ft to 6ft above the orlop platforms. While it had openings for hatches to allow access to the hold and orlop, it was a complete structural deck. On a warship with two gun decks this was the location of the bottom tier of guns. The guns were arranged

The long gun – smoothbored and muzzle loading – was the primary weapon of the warship during the American Revolution. This is a bronze French gun, now on display at the United States Navy Museum at Washington, DC. (USN)

in two rows running the length of the ship, a row pointing out of either side of the ship, and fired perpendicular to the ship's direction of travel.

On a warship with two or more gun decks, the lower deck was also used for crew accommodation, with the crew sleeping in hammocks slung between the guns. If a ship had only one gun deck, the lower deck was used primarily for lodging, and sometimes called the berth deck. Between 4ft and 7ft above the lower deck was the upper deck. It too ran the length of the ship, and was also a structural deck – in fact the main structural deck of a ship. It was the deck on which guns were always mounted. On the largest warships, there would be a third gun-carrying full deck above this deck. In that case, this second full deck became the middle deck and the third deck was the upper deck.

These decks were the full-length decks built into a ship. Above the upper deck were additional partial decks: the forecastle forward, and the quarterdeck in the after half of the ship. Sometimes, at the aftermost half of the quarterdeck was an additional deck above the quarterdeck called the poop. While substantial in appearance, these upper works were lightly built. They were intended to protect the ship's bow and stern from waves, offer greater visibility for those operating the ship, and provide space for accommodation on the decks below them – the commissioned and senior warrant officers on a warship, and privileged passengers on merchant craft were housed below the quarterdeck, while warrant officers such as the boatswain and carpenter slept below the forecastle.

The poop was the highest deck in a warship, on the after end of the quarterdeck. It was usually too light to take the weight of long guns, although it offered Marines an elevated platform from which to fire their muskets. (AC-HMM)

The forecastle was a platform from which the anchors and cables used to moor a ship were managed. The quarterdeck contained the ship's helm, the control for the rudder used to help turn the ship, and the station for the ship's command team, the captain and his immediate assistants. The poop provided shelter for the helmsman on the quarterdeck (on a sailing ship, the position most exposed to the elements was the stern) and as the ceiling for the captain's and admiral's cabins.

At the start of the 18th century the quarterdeck and forecastle were completely separate, requiring anyone wishing to travel from one to the other to climb down a ladder to the ship's waist (the upper deck between the quarterdeck and forecastle), and then up another once across the waist. By the middle of the century, the quarterdeck and forecastle were joined by gangways – lightly built passageways along the sides often no wider than required to allow a man's passage.

The main guns were housed on the two main decks. These were smoothbore cannon that fired an iron ball. The cannon were cast as a single piece of iron or bronze between 6ft and 10ft long, bored out at the muzzle end, with a solid breech. By the middle of the 18th century most naval artillery was iron due to the greater expense of bronze. Cost was important because a typical warship carried numerous guns. A small warship carried a dozen. The largest carried 100 or more. The average ship used in the line of battle carried 74 guns, while the standard cruising warships mounted between 24 and 48 guns.

The large numbers were necessary because guns of the day were inaccurate. On the rolling deck of a ship you were lucky to hit a ship-sized target 100yd away, even if you aimed properly. Additionally, solid shot was the standard ammunition for naval guns, which could only batter a target into submission. Explosive shells existed, but fuse technology was so primitive as to make these more dangerous to the ship that fired them than their target. Between the inherent inaccuracy of the naval cannon and the limited ability of solid shot to do damage, volume of fire determined battles. So ships fired broadsides of cannon – lining a deck with a row of guns – whenever possible.

The heaviest and largest guns were placed on the lower gun deck, while a lighter battery was placed on the upper gun deck. The quarterdeck carried an even lighter set of guns and often a pair of light guns were also placed on the forecastle. Through most of the 18th century the poop was generally too light to bear the weight of guns, although it provided a place to store the chicken coops that housed the ship's poultry. This mixed battery was dictated by structural and stability considerations. The further weight was from the waterline, the less stable a ship became. The iron guns then used were among the densest items a ship carried. All but the lightest guns weighed thousands of pounds, and even light guns weighed hundreds of pounds each. The lower tier of guns typically fired a round that weighed twice to three-halves the weight of the shot fired from the battery immediately above it. The barrel of the upper gun weighed 60–70 percent of the mass of the gun mounted immediately below it. However, this caused logistical problems, for each size of gun used a different-sized iron ball and gunpowder cartridge.

Ships were both powered and steered by wind. By the start of the 18th century the standard ocean-going ship used three masts. The central main mast was generally placed near the ship's longitudinal center of buoyancy, the ship's pivot point. Because of a hull's shape this was typically 5 to 10 percent of the ship's length aft of amidships. The fore mast was typically placed one-quarter of a ship's length from the bow of the ship, and the after mast – called the mizzen – was located one-fifth of the distance from the stern. The center or main mast was the largest mast. The fore mast was typically four-fifths the height of the main mast, while the mizzen mast was two-thirds the length of the main mast.

These masts were divided into two or three parts. From lowest to highest these sections were the lower mast, the top mast and the topgallant mast. The lower mast of the fore and main mast was anchored on the ship's keel in a mast step at the very bottom of the hull. The mast step for the mizzen was usually set on the lower gun deck. Lower masts were permanently fixed, guyed by a triangle of lines. The lines running aft and to the side were called shrouds. The lines running forward were called stays. Topmasts were mounted on the lower masts, fixed ahead of the lower mast by connections at the top and bottom of the overlap between the two mast sections, called the doubling. The topgallant mast was attached to the top of the topmast in a similar fashion. The upper and topgallant masts were also guyed by their own stays and shrouds.

The topsails were the main driving sails of ships of the era. These topmen are shown here furling the main topsail. Handling the sails was an all-hands job. (AC)

The reason for this sectional approach lay in the limitations of wood. It was difficult to find a single piece of wood greater than 100ft in length. Rather than accept the maximum length of a tree trunk as the limit for a mast's length, shipwrights lengthened the mast by attaching a second, and then a third section to the lower mast. Eventually, a fourth mast, the royal, would be attached to the topgallant. By then the law of diminishing returns set in, yielding an almost trivial increase in speed from the effort of adding another mast.

Each mast was rigged with sails. Two types of sails were carried: square sails and fore-and-aft sails. The square sails (which were actually trapezoidal) were the main driving sails that moved a ship, and were suspended under a spar mounted perpendicular to the length of the ship. The fore-and-aft sails were either hung from the mast stays or from a gaff boom behind a mast. While these contributed to a ship's speed, their main purpose was to assist in turning the ship. The main steering sails were the triangular jibs that hung off the stays that ran from the fore mast to the jib boom and the trapezoidal gaff sail behind the mizzen mast. Trimming these sails so that the wind's power pushed sideways allowed a ship's crew to pivot a ship about the mainmast.

This configuration yielded a ship that was fast, weatherly, and stable when the ship was at least 150ft long. This was the size of a ship-of the-line, the largest warship used. These were too large to use as cruisers. For patrolling, convoy escort, and commerce

BONHOMME RICHARD

Length between perpendiculars: 145ft
Length of keel: 126ft
Extreme breadth: 36ft 8in
Depth of hold: 15ft
Draft: 17ft 6in
Displacement: 998 tons
Complement: 380 officers

Armament: six 18-pounder smoothbore cannon, 16 "new model" and 12 "old model" 12-pounder smoothbore cannon, six 8-pounder smoothbore cannon
Launched: November 28, 1765 (as *Duc de Duras*), L'Orient, France
Acquired: February 4, 1779 (as *Bonhomme Richard*)
Fate: sunk in combat, off Flamborough Head, September 25, 1779

Built as *Duc de Duras* for *La Compagnie des Indies* (known in Britain as the French East India Company), *Bonhomme Richard* was one of nine 900-ton Indiamen designed by and constructed under the supervision of Antoine Groignard. As *Duc de Duras*, it made two voyages to the Indies before *La Compagnie des Indies* went bankrupt in 1769. The ship was adopted by the French Crown in 1769, fitted out as a troop transport, and carried 400 soldiers to Île de France (today's Mauritius). In 1771 it was again transferred to civilian hands; it was rebuilt in 1772 and made a fourth Indies voyage. It had another overhaul in 1778, when its owner outfitted the ship to serve as either a privateer or an armed transport. When Benjamin Franklin began searching for a suitable command for Jones, the ship was available. It was purchased by the French for the United States, and renamed *Bonhomme Richard*, after the pseudonym used by Franklin for his almanac. While the ship could have carried as many as 64 guns, a shortage of suitable artillery led to it being armed with only 42 guns. It made only one voyage under the Stars and Stripes, sinking the day after the battle of Flamborough Head.

raiding, smaller warships were more effective. While the hulls could be shrunk, maintaining the same ratios, people could not. A certain minimum deck height was required to allow humans to work efficiently, especially when the work involved hard physical labor. Placing gun decks much closer than 5ft apart made them unworkable.

The result was that as the hull got shorter, two-deckers became proportionately taller. Increasing the height above the waterline gave more exposed surface for wind to work on. This made a ship less handy. It was easier for the wind to push the ship sideways, which made the ship more difficult to steer and turn, a characteristic mariners termed "crank." To reduce this height, shipwrights dropped the lower deck closer to the keel. This reduced the size of the hold, which reduced hold storage. It also brought the lower gunports closer to the waterline, which made it difficult to use the lower guns in rough seas.

Two-decker warships with as few as 32 guns were built in the late 17th and early 18th century, but these ships were slow, crank, and "tender" (unstable). The bottoms of the lower gunports were only 3½ft above the waterline. By the middle of the 18th century, the single-deck frigate replaced the two-deck cruiser. With frigates, shipwrights dropped the lower gun deck to just above the waterline, and moved the guns formerly mounted on the lower deck to the upper gun deck. While a frigate carried fewer guns, it could use its heavy guns in all weathers, and sail rings around the small two-decker. By the start of the 1770s only two types of two-deckers smaller than ships-of-the-line still existed: the Indiaman and the 44-gun to 54-gun two-decker warship.

THE INDIAMAN

Indiamen were among the largest merchant ships built in Europe during the 18th century. The smallest Indiamen were 500 tons while the largest were as big as ships-of-the-line, displacing up to 1,400 tons. Ships that simply sailed across the Atlantic typically displaced between 100 and 250 tons – and often were as small as 50 tons. By the middle of the 18th century, most Indiamen ran between 800 and 1,100 tons, the size of two-decker warships too small to stand in the line of battle. Towards the end of the 18th century many two-decker warships originally built as Indiamen were often purchased by navies and converted to warships.

The reason for building such large, warship-type merchant ships lay in the trade in which they engaged. The East Indies – a term that encompassed the Indian subcontinent, Sri Lanka, the numerous islands between the Indian and Pacific Ocean, and China – held some of the most valuable cargoes in the world. The hunt for spices had originally prompted the development of the trans-oceanic ship. Silk, fine china, tea, and coffee were other valuable East Indies products sought by Europe. The Indies were also a long way from Europe. A round trip could take over a year, but the financial return was enough to make the time spent worthwhile.

The length of the voyage required carrying large quantities of the food, water, and supplies needed to keep sailors healthy over a long voyage – at least six months' worth per man. The voyage also took a ship over some of the world's most lawless areas. Pirates were threats even during peacetime. To protect both ship and freight, ship owners and captains armed the ships making this voyage, preferably heavily. Of course, guns required men to service them, increasing the crew size – and storage requirements for the additional food and water required for these extra men.

Finally, these ships also traveled through some of the world's roughest waters. In addition to the hazards of the North Atlantic in winter, to reach the Indies a ship had to pass through the Roaring Forties, the stormy belt between 40 degrees and 50 degrees South latitude. There, with the oceans largely uninterrupted by any land, wind and waves built up into virtually continuous gale-force winds and mountainous seas. Throw in Indian Ocean typhoons and the Atlantic hurricane belt, and you had a passage that required a sturdy ship.

A ship that met these requirements and still had space for cargo – both outbound and inbound – was necessarily large and well built. The resulting vessel was called an East Indiaman, or simply as an Indiaman. While the Indiamen that are best known today were those built for Britain's Honourable East India Company, virtually every European nation had its own company licensed to trade with the East Indies, and built their own versions of the Indiaman.

All Indiamen were similar to two-decker warships in both design and appearance, as the design yielded characteristics needed for both functions – space for stores, accommodation for large numbers of people, and the structural ability to stand

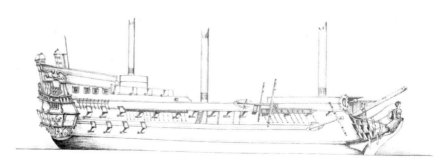

A French East Indiaman. The high superstructure of an East Indiaman is clearly shown. (AC)

punishment. Both Indiamen and two-decker warships had the basic internal design – two full decks plus a forecastle, quarterdeck, and poop, although Indiamen frequently skipped adding orlop platforms to increase the hold.

Indiamen carried a smaller crew than warships, and much storage space was given over to cargo rather than crew stores and ammunition. The storms of the Roaring Forties, typhoons, and hurricanes that Indiamen faced placed different stresses on a ship than the round-shot warships received in combat. Yet Indiamen were more similar to warships than to Newcastle colliers, West Indies sugar traders, or Liverpool slavers.

There were differences. An Indiaman's scantlings – the wood used to build the ship's hull – while heavier than used in a conventional merchantman, was lighter than what would have been used for a ship intended as a warship. While the lower deck of an Indiaman was pierced for gunports, there was generally half the number of gunports on the Indiaman's lower deck than on a similarly sized warship's. An Indiaman typically carried no guns on the lower deck, using that space for cargo too delicate for storage in the hold – porcelain and silk, for example – or for passenger accommodation. Indiamen also tended to have larger quarterdecks and poops than a purpose-built warship. The extra space yielded was used to accommodate first-class passengers.

Another major difference between Indiamen and warships was the number of guns carried. While a warship would have two full gun decks and guns on the upper works, Indiamen typically carried only a single battery of guns, mounted on the upper gun deck. Even that deck typically carried fewer guns than its naval counterpart. Whereas a ship in naval service would carry 30 guns on its upper deck, the Indiaman would

HMS *SERAPIS*

Length between perpendiculars: 140ft 2in
Length of keel: 115ft 7in
Extreme breadth: 38ft 1.5in
Depth of hold: 15ft
Draft: 16ft 3in
Displacement: 889 tons

Complement: 280 officers, men, and Marines
Armament: 20 18-pounder smoothbore cannon, 22 9-pounder
    smoothbore cannon, two 6-pounder smoothbore cannon
Launched: Randall & Co., Rotherhithe, England, March 3, 1779
Commissioned: May 5, 1779
Fate: burned off Madagascar in French service, July 1781

Serapis was one of 19 Roebuck-class 44-gun two-deckers ordered and built during the American Revolutionary Wars. Based on a 1769 design by Sir Thomas Slade, these ships were low-draft ships intended for use on the shallow North and Baltic Seas and for coastal defense. *Serapis* had only a brief career with the Royal Navy, as it had been in commission less than six months prior to the battle of Flamborough Head, when it was captured. At the time – as intended by its design – it was escorting a Baltic convoy, returning to London. Following its capture by the Continental Navy, diplomatic efforts by Britain led to its transfer to the French Navy. Recommissioned, it was sent to reinforce French naval forces in India. In July 1781, while off Madagascar en route to India, an overturned lantern in the spirit room started a fire that destroyed the ship.

mount between 20 and 24, leaving the ports closest to the bow and stern empty. Indiamen did not need bow chasers – guns carried in the bow and firing forward – as they would not be pursuing enemy ships, and guns in cabins took up space desired by passengers. The Indiaman's broadside of ten to 12 guns, typically 12-pounder smoothbores, was adequate for its main purpose – discouraging pirates from attacking.

While the Indiaman, when sailing as a merchant vessel, was not a warship, it could easily be converted into a two-decker. The missing gunports on the lower deck and orlop platforms could be added with a few days' work. Add a full battery of guns on both gun decks and the upper works and you had a warship mounting between 44 and 56 guns. It might not stand up to the same type of punishment as a purpose-built warship in a pitched battle, but relatively little time was spent in stand-up sea fights. Your converted merchantman was an adequate convoy escort against most privateers, provided extra guns for blockade duty and could serve as a flagship on a remote station that did not require a ship-of-the-line.

Or – as in the case of *Bonhomme Richard* – an Indiaman could be turned into a powerful privateer.

THE TWO-DECKER WARSHIP

The Baltic powers, the Netherlands, and Britain built two-deckers for their navies throughout the 18th century. Today it is easy to question the need for the two-decker, or perhaps the need to construct purpose-built 44-gun to 56-gun warships rather than converting Indiamen to serve that function. After all, it was too small and too weak to stand in the line of battle, and too slow to catch fast privateers and cruisers. Seemingly,

Frigates, such as USS *Confederacy* shown here, replaced the small two-decker as cruisers and scouts. (USN)

its roles were better served by ships-of-the-line or frigates. Yet through the middle to end of the 18th century a role remained for the naval two-decker. It was only after the 24-pounder frigate emerged during the early years of the 19th century that the two-decker was abandoned. Despite their relative weakness and slowness, two-deckers did have utility.

The standard two-decker mounted a main battery of 18-pounder cannon. Occasionally, large two-deckers carried a 24-pounder main battery. Even the smallest ship-of-the-line, rated at 64 guns, carried a main battery of 24-pounder guns, while the standard 74-gun ship-of-the-line mounted a lower battery of 32-pounder smoothbores, as did larger ships-of-the-line, including three-deckers. But because they were smaller, two-deckers could sail in waters too shallow for ships-of-the-line to sail safely. The shoals off the Dutch coast, the southern shores of the North Sea, and the Baltic gave the two-decker a utility they lacked in the mid-Atlantic or Pacific. In shoal waters a 74-gun ship-of-the-line might outgun a two-decker, but often could not close range to catch the smaller ship. On the other hand, the two-decker could rule shallow waters because it could outgun anything else that could sail in those waters. In confined seas, a frigate could not make best use of its speed, especially if coasts constrained movement at its best point of sailing.

Another advantage of the two-decker was that it was economical of crew. A 74-gun ship-of-the-line took 650 men to man fully. A 44-gun two-decker required only 280 to 300 men. Even assuming that the average 74-gun vessel went to sea with a crew of only 580 to 600, you could still crew two 44-gun ships for the manpower it took to outfit one ship-of-the-line. While that ship-of-the-line could probably beat both two-deckers in a stand-up fight, it could not be in two places at the same time. Often having two fighting ships available was more important than having one more powerful warship.

A third reason why two-deckers continued to be used in place of ships-of-the-line or frigates was that while a two-decker was smaller than a ship-of-the-line, it was considerably larger than the frigates of the early 1770s. Many distant stations consisted of a squadron of frigates, small patrol warships, and a flagship. Carrying an admiral or commodore and his staff aboard a frigate led to cramped quarters. Since much of a flag officer's responsibilities were administrative, requiring time in port, using a frigate as a flagship also tied up a valuable frigate – generally the largest one in the squadron.

Sending a ship-of-the-line to distant (and often unimportant) stations to serve as flagship weakened the main battle line to which the ship would otherwise have been assigned. Instead, a two-decker could be sent as flagship. It had enough space to provide quarters for the flag and his staff, took fewer men to operate, and freed a ship-of-the-line for service in a battle squadron. Additionally, while a two-decker provided more firepower than that period's frigates, it was not so great that its broadside would be missed in a battle line. If the flagship stayed in port until it grounded on the beef bones tossed overboard by its crew, better that often-rumored but rarely achieved fate occur to a two-decker than a ship-of-the line.

A two-decker was also a superb convoy escort. It was larger than most privateers, and could at least match even a large naval frigate that might attack a convoy. It could not outsail a fast cruiser, but it could outsail any merchantman in its convoy. Thus while it could not chase down an attacking raider, it could run down and recapture any prizes taken. While frigates could (and did) escort convoys, there were always too few frigates. Using them as escorts meant they could not be used for scouting or raiding. Additionally, a frigate escort *could* catch a cruiser raiding a convoy. Sometimes frigate captains became so intent on taking a prize that they forgot their primary goal of protecting their convoy. A two-decker captain – who knew pursuit was likely fruitless – was less easily tempted.

Finally, two-deckers were easily converted to use as transports. The Royal Navy often had a temporary need to move troops to support an invasion. Striking a two-decker's main battery and stowing the guns in the hold quickly provided space to transport a battalion of troops. Once the troops were unloaded, the guns could be remounted and the ship again became a warship. Other nations, particularly the French, were forced to use frigates as fast transports. Additionally, this capability meant that a two-decker was useful as a stores ship once it was too worn-out to be used as a warship, giving the ship a second life less possible with ships-of-the-line or frigates.

One result of this utility was that the Royal Navy continued using two-deckers much later than other deep-water navies. Because converted merchantmen were inherently weaker warships than purpose-built ships, the Royal Navy continued ordering two-decker warships throughout the 18th century, and into the first decades of the 19th century.

One period of revival of building Royal Navy two-deckers occurred during the American Revolutionary Wars. As with the Baltic Sea, the American coastline had an abundance of shallow-draught water that increased the need for two-deckers. This included the Roebuck class, of which 20 were built – and one of which, *Serapis*, fought at Flamborough Head.

THE STRATEGIC SITUATION

By 1779 Britain had been at war with its American colonies for four years. What began as colonial protests against Parliamentary taxes in 1774 exploded into armed resistance the following year. When Britain's King George III sided with Parliament, declaring the colonists to be in a state of rebellion, the colonists refused to submit. Instead, they chose to dissolve the political ties connecting them to England, declaring independence. Refusing to accept this unilateral assertion, in 1776 the British sent an army to North America to put down what they viewed as a rebellion. As Britain saw it, independence was only actively supported by a third of the rebelling colonies' population and was actively opposed by almost as large a fraction of colonists.

Yet over the next two years those actively supporting independence proved more energetic than those opposing it. The United States, as these colonies now styled themselves, raised armies (states raised their own armies in addition to the one established by the national government) and created a navy. While these forces were frequently beaten by the British military and naval forces, they proved remarkably tenacious. Every time the colonists got beaten, they simply re-formed elsewhere, and challenged British authority once again.

Moreover, while the British frequently beat these colonial insurgents, the Continentals did occasionally win. They forced the British to evacuate Boston, Massachusetts; held Charleston, South Carolina against a British amphibious assault; and destroyed British brigades at Trenton and Princeton in New Jersey. Finally, in October 1777, they forced a British army to surrender at Saratoga in upstate New York.

Until Saratoga, the American Revolutionary Wars were a relatively minor affair for Britain. While tens of thousands of soldiers had been sent to the New World, by Continental standards this was small beer. Additionally, the expansion of the Royal Navy involved only a very limited mobilization. The Continental Navy was a minor irritant, made up of a handful of frigates and a dozen or so sloops-of-war. Continental privateers – privately owned warships authorized by a Continental government to capture prizes – were more of a problem, but even these could be controlled by a limited number of light cruisers, rather than ships-of-the-line.

Some Royal Navy assets were required to protect communications and move supplies, but again, ships large enough to stand in the line-of-battle were not required. Indeed, the two-decker was an ideal ship for the Navy's responsibilities between 1775 and 1778, leading to a revival of that class by the Royal Navy.

This was not to say that Continental naval effort was uniformly futile. A small collection of armed sloops established by George Washington in 1775 made significant contributions to the Continental victory at Boston. The prizes they took supplied Washington's army, and encouraged the British withdrawal. A Continental Navy squadron under Esek Hopkins raided New Providence in the Bahamas in 1776. John Paul Jones took the sloop-of-war *Ranger* into the Irish Sea in 1778, capturing the British sloop-of-war *Drake* on the cruise. Those efforts, while gallant and intrepid, were simply irritants.

Everything changed following Saratoga. Britain had decisively defeated France in the Seven Years' War of 1756 to 1763 following a set of brilliant naval victories and amphibious landings. France wanted to avenge this humiliating defeat. France saw British preoccupation in North America as an opportunity to regain some of the earlier losses, especially when Saratoga showed that the rebelling colonials had staying power.

France signed a treaty of alliance with the United States in February 1778, recognizing the colonies as a sovereign nation. The French did so knowing that their recognition was unacceptable to Britain. Britain declared war on France in March 1778,

Benjamin Franklin signing the Treaty of Amity and Commerce with France. When France signed this, it made war with Britain inevitable. (LoC)

after the treaty was made known to Britain. The rebellion in North America was now a major war that would be fought globally.

Having European involvement changed the naval war. European allies provided the United States with a base close to their enemy's home. Continental warships and privateers could openly operate out of France. It also brought them a source of supply for both their armies and their naval forces, albeit a generally parsimonious source. France was more interested in punishing Britain than in aiding the United States. Additionally, having a European ally with a strong navy allowed the Continental government to focus on its army and de-emphasize its navy. No new naval warships were authorized by the Continental Congress after France entered the war, and only a handful of those still under construction were eventually completed.

For Britain, the situation became dire. From March 1778 onward Britain was fighting for its own survival as much as it was fighting to retain its rebelling North American colonies. France had a formidable navy. It had spent much of the 1760s and early 1770s building up its navy, reforming naval administration, and replacing the ships lost during the Seven Years' War. When France mobilized its fleet, Britain did likewise, and focused its attention on the French threat across the narrow Channel. Soon both nations had large fleets of ships-of-the-line facing each other. Initially each navy had a fleet only in the Channel, but both nations dispatched fleets to the Caribbean, the Mediterranean, and eventually the East Indies, either to gain an advantage in those theaters or in response to the other nation's threat.

Britain was also faced with the task of expanding, outfitting, and supplying its fleet. The need for expansion would become more critical in April 1779, when Spain also declared war on Britain. In the 1770s and 1780s Britain was largely self-sufficient. It had one of the world's largest iron industries, allowing the British to manufacture the artillery and iron fittings required for their navy. They still possessed sufficient oak to build warships. Local sources of pine were nearing exhaustion, however. Pine provided masts used for propulsion, as well as turpentine and pitch, used to waterproof wooden ships. Furthermore, the Royal Navy's need for new masts was exacerbated because the supply of masts had been allowed to dwindle following the Seven Years' War as an economy measure.

Prior to the American Revolution, the Royal Navy's major sources of pine lay in Britain's North American colonies, particularly those in New England, the heart of the rebellion. Their Canadian colonies, gained during the Seven Years' War, provided an alternative source of these naval stores, but at the time of the American Revolution these had not been developed. With France allied against Britain, the remaining sources of masts, pitch, turpentine, and other naval stores lay in the Baltic states – Sweden, Denmark, and Russia.

To assure delivery of these critical strategic materials, British merchantmen sailing to and from the Baltic sailed in convoy. Royal Navy warships escorted these convoys to protect them from enemy warships and privateers. As Britain could not afford to weaken its line-of-battle in the face of the French naval threat and needed its frigates for fleet scouting, these convoys were usually escorted by two-deckers and sloops-of-war.

The frigate action between the French *Belle Poule* and British *Arethusa* in July 1778 marked the opening of active hostilities between Great Britain and France. (AC)

Although the United States de-emphasized its naval efforts after French entry into the war, it never completely abandoned them. As long as it had warships – or could purchase new vessels from European powers – it was willing to maintain a small navy. While British diplomacy had checked Continental efforts to purchase warships from neutral powers, as European powers became allied with the United States their shipyards and reserve fleets became available to the Americans.

After French entry into the war, the United States was no longer interested in building a conventional navy based on ships capable of standing in the line of battle. Rather, they wanted a navy that could serve to raid and harry British shipping to North America. Another strategic goal for the United States was to force Britain to commit more of the Royal Navy's light units in British home waters. Every cruiser committed to guard Britain and Ireland was a ship unavailable to prowl American coastal estuaries. Thus, in 1778 and 1779, efforts were made to send Continental warships to raid British waters.

The most successful raid prior to 1779 was the cruise of *Ranger* in the Irish Sea in April 1778. Its material accomplishments were relatively minor – *Ranger* captured three merchant ships, one small British warship, and launched a successful raid on the British port of Whitehaven. Its moral impact was much higher, however. It was the first time a British warship had been captured in equal combat with a Continental warship. While the daring raid on Whitehaven was militarily insignificant, it created calls for increased local defenses throughout Britain.

Ranger's commander, John Paul Jones, was promoted following the cruise, but remained unemployed thereafter, as attempts to find a suitable command for him proved unsuccessful. However, in early 1779 he was given command of a former French East Indiaman, and named commodore of a small squadron of Continental and French warships. By mid-summer he was ready to repeat his earlier cruise – only this time he planned to sail around all of England, with a squadron, rather than a single sloop-of-war.

The capture of HMS *Drake* by the Continental Navy sloop-of-war *Ranger* created an uproar in Britain and marked John Paul Jones as a captain to watch. (MOA-UM)

TECHNICAL SPECIFICATIONS

Evenly matched battles are rare in naval history, yet the battle between *Bonhomme Richard* and *Serapis* was one that pitted two reasonably equal opponents against one another. Materially, *Serapis* had several advantages. It was newer, had a larger broadside, and was a handier ship than *Bonhomme Richard*. *Serapis* could sail faster and was more maneuverable. Against those advantages, *Bonhomme Richard* was a larger ship, which allowed it to soak up more punishment, and provided a height advantage. It also carried a much larger contingent of Marines, seagoing soldiers that were as much a part of a ship's armament and combat capability as its great guns. These helped reduce the advantage held by *Serapis*.

There were also operational considerations that reduced *Serapis's* material edge. *Serapis* had a convoy to defend. To prevent *Bonhomme Richard* from reaching the merchantmen it guarded, *Serapis* had to forfeit much of its advantage in maneuverability and speed. The advantages and drawbacks possessed by each combatant in the contest at Flamborough Head can be best appreciated through an examination of both ships in terms of structure, armament, and propulsion.

STRUCTURE

While both *Bonhomme Richard* and *Serapis* were two-deckers, *Bonhomme Richard* was built as an Indiaman, while *Serapis* was designed and built as a warship. This affected their hull structure in several ways.

As an Indiaman, *Bonhomme Richard* was designed primarily to carry cargo. When *Duc de Duras* was built it had no orlop, in order to provide the maximum hold volume. As *Bonhomme Richard*, the orlop had been added, although it is unclear whether it had been added when the French Navy purchased *Duc de Duras* in 1770 or as part of the general refit when it was converted to a warship. It was larger than *Serapis*, 10ft longer and displacing 110 tons more than the British warship. It also had a larger superstructure. *Bonhomme Richard*'s quarterdeck took up a larger percentage of the overall length of the ship than did *Serapis*'s. As was typical with ships intended to carry passengers, *Bonhomme Richard* was built with a sizable poop to provide accommodation for important passengers. *Serapis* was built without a poop. The toplofty superstructure gave *Bonhomme Richard*'s Marines a higher and larger platform from which to fight. It also gave the wind a larger surface to act upon. This made it less maneuverable and harder to handle in lively winds.

The difference in intended purpose also affected the structural strength and integrity of both ships. Despite its larger size a ship built as an Indiaman was built with lighter scantlings than a ship built as a warship, its frames being smaller than those intended for a warship of the same size. *Serapis* was built to withstand the shock of firing broadsides of heavy guns over long periods of time. While *Duc de Duras* was designed to carry a heavier battery than *Serapis*, it was not expected to be routinely outfitted with both gun decks fully armed, and its builders anticipated that whatever battles it did fight would be brief.

HMS *Diomede*, launched in 1780, was a sister-ship of *Serapis*. It is shown with HMS *Centurion*, a 50-gun two-decker, fighting French warships in 1794. (AC)

By contrast, *Serapis* was built for service in the Royal Navy, and its designer anticipated the possibility that a ship of its class might have to stand in the line-of-battle. As a result it was built with heavier framing, to absorb the punishment of a sea fight that lasted hours, as well as to endure the punishment that the recoil of its own guns would mete out to the hull.

Bonhomme Richard was also significantly older. Launched in 1765, it had made four round trips to the Indies, enduring the strains imposed by the Roaring Forties eight times, as well as 14 years of immersion in salt water and exposure to damp air that promoted rot. When refitted, obviously rotten wood was replaced, but weakened wood often went undetected. Combined with its smaller scantlings, it meant that when *Duc de Duras* was converted to *Bonhomme Richard*, the ship was too weak to carry a full battery of guns. Iron knees were added to the hull during the refit to reinforce the lower gun deck and strengthen the ship. By contrast, *Serapis*, built the previous year, had all of the structural integrity of a new ship built from seasoned wood.

One real structural advantage *Serapis* possessed was hidden below the waterline. It was coppered. The underwater hull was plated with thin, overlapping copper sheets. These protected the hull against shipworm, and discouraged marine growth. Due to its recent construction *Serapis* was one of the Royal Navy's early coppered ships, and may have been the first warship encountered by the Continental Navy to be so equipped. Even though *Bonhomme Richard* was less than a year out of the dockyard at the time of the battle, its hull would already have been hosting an underwater garden of sea plants on its hull, further slowing the former Indiaman, while *Serapis* would have had the advantage of a clean hull.

ARMAMENT

Bonhomme Richard and *Serapis* were armed with similar main weapons – smoothbore muzzle-loading cannon. The size, quantity, and quality of their guns differed, but not how they operated.

On its lower gun deck *Serapis* had a main battery of 20 18-pounder smoothbore cannon, ten on each side of the ship. The 18-pounder's barrel was 9½–10½ft long, and

Small swivel cannon firing 1lb balls or clusters of musket balls were mounted on bulwarks or in the fighting tops as anti-personal weapons. This Revolutionary-era swivel was recovered from a ship sunk in Penobscot Bay. (USN)

it weighed 4,200–4,300lb. An 18-pounder long gun fired a solid 5.04in-diameter iron ball that weighed 18lb. At a 3-degree elevation, it would throw a ball 1,180yd. Using its maximum 6lb charge of gunpowder a ball fired from an 18-pounder would penetrate 42in of oak. In the American Revolutionary Wars it was considered a heavy gun, albeit the lightest of what was then considered heavy artillery. Although the first frigates carrying 18-pounder long guns appeared during this war, the 18-pounder was primarily used on two-deckers and ships-of-the-line. It typically comprised the lower battery of two-deckers and the upper battery of a ship-of-the-line.

Serapis also mounted 22 9-pounder smoothbore cannon on its upper deck. A 9-pounder was as long as an 18-pounder, but significantly lighter. Its barrel weighed

COPPER BOTTOMS

The copper bottom of a British warship model. Coppering was used almost exclusively by Britain during the American Revolution. (AC-HMM)

One of the greatest enemies of saltwater sailors was the teredo worm. Commonly called the shipworm, the teredo worm ate submerged wood, and could turn the unprotected underwater hull of an oceangoing ship into a leaky sponge in less than a year.

The solution – covering the underwater hull with thin sheets of copper – was first proposed in 1708, but the first copper-plated ship would not emerge until 1762. That trial showed copper not only poisoned the teredo, but it prevented hull marine growth, too. Coppered ships were not only proof against shipworm, they sailed faster. But other experiments in the 1760s revealed that copper, when it came in contact with iron fittings in the hull, destroyed the iron through galvanic corrosion. These problems were not solved until the 1770s.

In early 1779 the Royal Navy ordered all ships larger than 32 guns to be coppered when they entered drydock. *Serapis*, launched in April, 1779, benefited. It was coppered when outfitted, one of the reasons that it could outsail *Bonhomme Richard*. Along with the carronade, copper-bottoming was one of two major naval innovations by the Royal Navy during the American Revolutionary Wars.

THE GREAT GUNS

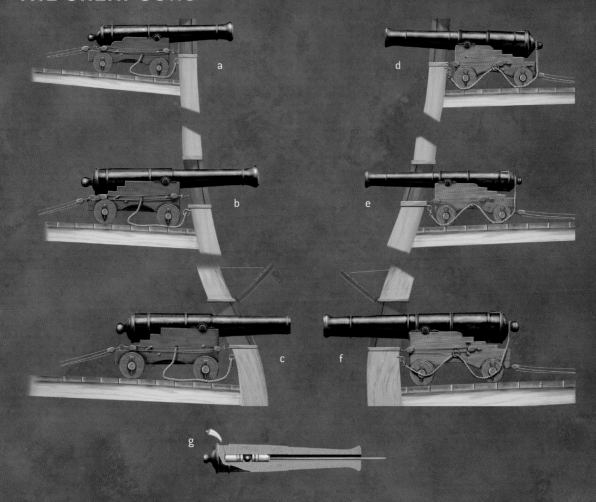

The main hitting power of a sailing warship of the American Revolutionary Wars lay in its great guns – iron cannon mounted on trucked carriages. While an ordnance revolution that dramatically changed naval artillery began during the American Revolutionary Wars, at Flamborough Head the combatants used guns little changed from those warships had been using for over 150 years.

As can be seen by the cutaway illustration, a naval cannon was a solid cast-iron cylinder bored out at the muzzle end. A touchhole was drilled through the top of the cannon to the bore, near the breech to allow ignition of powder charge loaded at the back of the cannon's bore, which propelled a solid iron ball, when ignited. A disk of wadding was placed at either end of the cannonball, to hold it in place. Charge and ball would be individually driven home with the rammer. The great guns at Flamborough Head were:

Bonhomme Richard:
(a) "New Model" 8-pounder (upper gun deck)
(b) "Old Model" 12-pounder (lower gun deck)
(g – cutaway) "New Model" 12-pounder (lower gun deck)
(c) "Old Model" 18-pounder (lower gun deck)

Serapis:
(d) 6-pounder (upper gun deck)
(e) 12-pounder (lower gun deck)
(f) 18-pounder (lower gun deck)

A sailor from the American colonies. While native-born Americans were always the largest fraction of the crew of Continental warships, sailors born in Britain and Ireland also formed large parts of Continental warship crews. (AC)

2,500–2,600lb. It used a 3lb charge, but had a slightly longer range than the heavier 18-pounder long gun – 1,200yd. Its ball was 4in in diameter. The 9-pounder had less penetration than the 18-pounder, but it could still punch through the upper works of a wooden warship. The "long nine" was a favorite gun in the Royal Navy. Since the diameter of its bore was 80 percent of that the 18-pounder, but its barrel was just as long, it had a higher caliber (ratio of length to width of the bore). This yielded a phenomenally accurate weapon at long ranges, and the 9-pounder was frequently used as a chase gun.

Finally, *Serapis* had a pair of 6-pounder long guns on its quarterdeck. These were both shorter and lighter than its other guns. The 6-pounder's barrel was 6½ft long and it weighed just over 2,000lb. It fired a 3½in ball, using a 2lb charge. While the guns had some anti-personnel value and were useful for knocking down rigging, they were not likely to sink anything but the very smallest ships.

While *Serapis* carried the full complement of 44 guns for which it was designed, *Bonhomme Richard* could potentially have carried 64. Instead it mounted only 42, six of which were more dangerous to its own crew than to the enemy. *Bonhomme Richard*, like *Serapis*, was intended to carry 18-pounders on its lower gun deck. Potentially it could have carried 28, but it was pierced for only 14 gunports due to concern for the effect of the guns. The United States depended upon France for artillery, and the French Navy had its own need for 18-pounders. Only six were available for *Bonhomme Richard*. These had been obtained from *Bonhomme Richard*'s 1778 owner, who had purchased guns surplus to the needs of the French Navy. In theory, these guns had the same capabilities as the British 18-pounders, but they were deficient. They were old guns, cast prior to 1766, and the iron had become brittle with age. At least one burst during the battle. After Jones took command, he remounted these guns, placing them aft, to improve *Bonhomme Richard*'s trim. He had an extra gunport installed between the two aftermost gunports, yielding a spacing between guns akin to that used on warships, rather than Indiamen.

Bonhomme Richard's main punch was provided by the 28 12-pounder long guns on its upper deck. The 12-pounder fired an iron ball 4.4in in diameter. With a 6lb charge it could send a ball 1,190yd when elevated 3 degrees. As with the 18-pounders, these

A long gun with the tackle and equipment used to point and fire it. The sailor is holding a handspike. (BOOS)

guns were what remained after French Navy needs had been met. As a result, 12 of the 12-pounder guns were "Old Model" guns with 8½ft barrels that weighed 3,300lb, and 14 were "New Model" guns with 7½ft barrels that weighed 3,100lb. The older, heavier guns were probably placed aft to help trim *Bonhomme Richard*, which needed extra weight aft to make up for the missing cargo.

Finally, *Bonhomme Richard* carried eight 8-pounder "New Model" long guns on its quarterdeck. The barrels of these guns were 6ft 10in long, and they weighed 2,100lb. They fired 8lb balls that were just under 4in in diameter.

SAILS AND RIGGING

Bonhomme Richard and *Serapis* were full-rigged ships, with square sails set on three masts. Both ships relied on their topsails – the second sail from the bottom, which was attached to the topmasts – as the main driving sails. The courses – the sails set on the lower mast, which were set below the topsails – and the topgallants – square sails set on the lower part of the topgallant masts, which were above the topmasts – could be used to add speed when the ship was cruising.

In light winds, both ships could rig royal sails above the topgallants. These sails were not rigged on their own masts, as would frequently be the case in later years. Rather, they were set on the topgallant mast, hung from a yard placed above the topgallant sail. In very light airs, studding sails could be raised. These were strips of canvas that were hung from booms attached to the ends of the spars, one on either side of the sail to which they were being added.

Finally, in addition to the fore-and-aft sails mentioned previously, both *Bonhomme Richard* and *Serapis* had square sails, called spritsails, hung from the bowsprit – the boom projecting ahead of the ship. These were steering sails. By the time of the

35

HAND WEAPONS

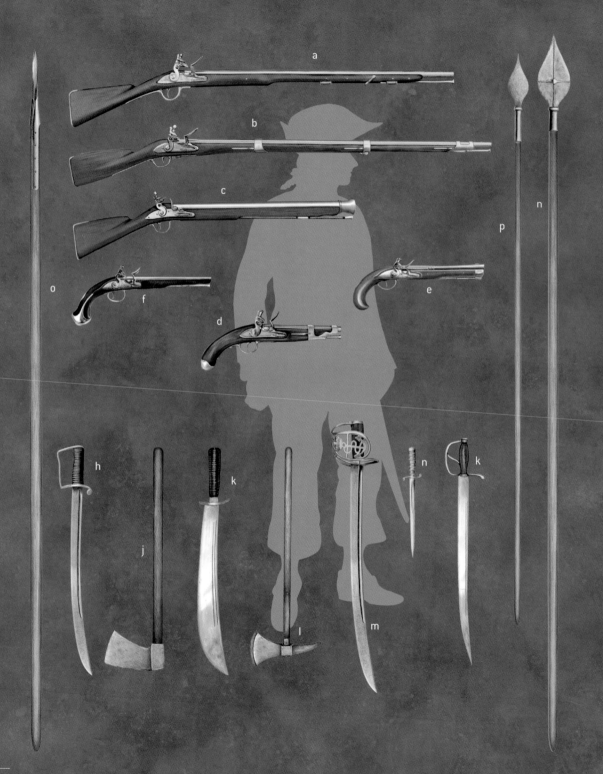

Because naval artillery of the sailing era rarely sank ships, most battles were ultimately decided by hand-to-hand combat, with the crew of one ship boarding a second in an attempt to take possession of it. Additionally, the range at which the artillery duel was conducted was often within range of the smoothbore muskets of the era. To supplement the efforts of the great guns ships would place musket-armed marksmen in the fighting tops and on the upper works. These men focused their fire on officers and gun crews, to reduce the fighting efficiency of their opponents.

The weapons used by the crews included: long arms used by marksmen – (a) British Sea Service Brown Bess musket, (b) French Sea Service Charleville musket, (c) French blunderbuss; pistols issued to boarders and officers – (d) French pistol, (e) Dutch pistol, (f) British pistol; and a wide assortment of edged weapons – (g) French naval cutlass, (h) British naval cutlass, (i) French boarding axe, (j) British boarding axe, (k) French naval sword, (l) British naval sword, (m) British naval dirk, (n) French boarding pike, (o) British boarding pike, (p) French half-pike.

Commissioned officers were armed with swords and pistols, midshipmen substituting a dirk for the sword, while sailors would either carry a pike or a pistol with a cutlass or boarding axe, depending upon the individual sailor's preference. Marines fought with muskets with fixed bayonets. As the pistols and muskets of the era were single-shot weapon that took time to reload, boarders carrying firearms also needed an edged weapon.

American Revolutionary Wars, they were being superseded by the more efficient jibs. They had not yet been abandoned entirely because captains did not yet completely trust the new-fangled jib (which had only appeared 50 or so years earlier). Besides, the spritsail spars were useful as spares, if a ship's masts and spars were damaged in battle.

The choice of sails used was a function of wind and wave conditions, and operational considerations. The greater the wind speed and the more sails that were set, the greater the strain on the masts and the rigging holding the masts in place. Light winds allowed every sail to be set, while under gale conditions, only reefed (shortened) topsails might be safe. Additionally, wind also tipped a ship to the downwind (or lee) side. Beyond a certain angle, a ship slowed, as the heeling effectively reduced a ship's draft and allowed it to be pushed sideways. Experienced captains understood the point at which this happened, and reduced sail area to avoid crossing it. They generally started with the uppermost sails – royals and topgallants – as these had the greatest effect on the ship's heeling.

Finally, in battle, a separate sail configuration was used. The courses would be brailed up – loosely bunched up under their spar to keep the canvas well away from the ship's deck. A set course was low enough that it could catch fire from burning gunpowder and wadding fired from the ship's own guns. Battles were generally fought under topsails with the outer jibs and mizzen gaff sails (used to help steer the ship) set.

In light winds the topgallants, and more rarely the royals, would also be set in combat. A captain had to be cautious in doing so because the extra strain they exerted on the rigging made it more likely that battle damage would bring down a mast, crippling a ship. One unusual aspect of the battle of Flamborough Head was that *Bonhomme Richard* actually set the topsail studding sails during the battle. It sailed so sluggardly that Jones accepted the risks posed by doing this.

THE COMBATANTS

Two-deckers carried crews of 250–400 men. Generally 220 to 240 of these would be mariners – the officers and sailors responsible for sailing the ship and working its guns. The rest would be Marines – sea soldiers – who fought with small arms. Although *Bonhomme Richard* was outfitted and manned in France rather than the United States, it drew upon the same pool of people that *Serapis* used for its sailors and a very similar set of people for its officers. Only the Marines aboard each ship came from different sources. Each group that fought at Flamborough Head – men, officers, and Marines – shaped the outcome of the battle.

THE MEN

In the 18th century, a full-rigged warship – whether a ship-of-the-line, a two-decker, or a frigate – was one of the world's most complicated machines. Nothing else had as many interconnected, moving parts, all of which had to be used properly, with a complex set of actions.

There was a role for the unskilled on a warship. Perhaps half of the activities on a ship could be done by them – hauling the lines to run guns in and out, pushing on capstan bars to raise anchor, or heaving on rigging lines while on deck. All of these tasks required supervision, from someone in the know – an experienced sailor. Although everything was operated by muscle power, brute strength alone was insufficient.

An experienced sailor "knew the ropes" (understood the ship's rigging) and could set, furl, and shorten a ship's sails, and operate the ship's rudder – whether using a tiller, or, as on two-decker, a ship's wheel. Men who could do that were said to be able to

A British Tar. Known popularly as Jack Tar or Jack Nastyface, he is shown in this 1779 cartoon beating up a Frenchman, a task Jack Tar embraced with greater enthusiasm than he did fighting his American cousins. (LoC)

handle, reef, and steer. They were prized by a ship's captain, regardless of nationality or whether the captain commanded a warship or a merchant vessel.

The most skilled seamen were the topmen, those who worked aloft in the rigging. They did some of the most necessary and dangerous work on a sailing ship, manipulating the sails, spars and upper masts, while anywhere from 50ft to several hundred feet above the deck. It was a young man's game. Topmen were often in their teens, and light, small men were preferred. Each mast's activities would be directed by the "captain of the top," an enlisted sailor, typically in his twenties. Older sailors usually worked on the deck, doing skilled work or supervising the unskilled.

While the life of a sailor of that time is considered hard today, it was not hard by the standards of the 18th-century working man. The work was physically demanding, but sailors, unlike laborers, were aided by machinery. The pay was generally better than a man could get ashore, and a sailor had a place to sleep and regular meals. Despite the wretched reputation of seagoing rations, sailors generally ate better than laborers or farmhands of the era, getting meat regularly, as well as a generous quantity of other food. It might be monotonous, but sailors rarely starved.

It was extremely dangerous. The hazards of the sea offered the greatest peril to a sailor, greater even than combat. Storms and shipwreck destroyed more ships and killed more men than combat, even during major wars. Disease took an even greater toll. While scurvy had finally been conquered in the decades prior to the American Revolution, epidemic diseases had not been. Typhus, yellow fever, and other tropical diseases killed more sailors than combat or the hazards of the sea combined.

However, in the mid-18th century, the life of a naval sailor was easier than that of a merchant sailor. Warships had large crews, allowing work to be distributed among more men. Navy discipline was less harsh than it would become during the

'WARE THE PRESS GANG

A press-gang at work in a London street in 1779. (LoC)

A major difference between the Royal and Continental Navies in manning their ships was that the Royal Navy used impressment, a misunderstood and often misrepresented form of maritime conscription. Continental crews were all volunteers. Impressment was limited by both custom and law.

Only "seamen, seafaring men, and persons whose occupations or calling are to work in vessels and boats upon the rivers" could legally be impressed. Landsmen could not lawfully be impressed, and during the American Revolutionary Wars *were* not. Impressment was intended to provide the Royal Navy with trained mariners. Filling a ship with unwilling miners or ploughmen failed to do that.

The system worked — as long as wars did not last much longer than three years. Three years was the traditional length of a commission for a warship, after which its crew was discharged from service. The naval phase of the American Revolutionary Wars only lasted from 1779 through 1782, which meant that most men involuntarily serving could expect to be pressed once, and serve one three-year commission on a warship before their services were no longer needed.

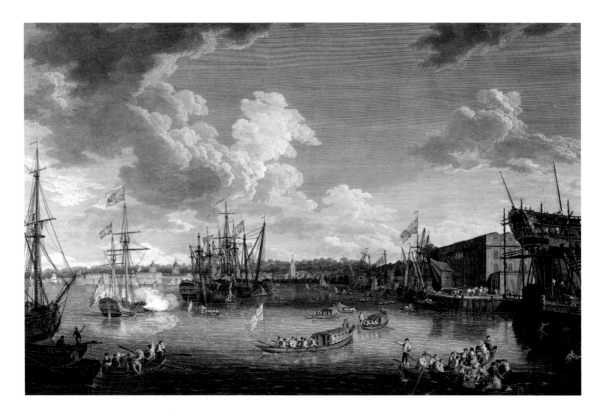

Napoleonic era. Navies, including the Royal Navy, granted sailors shore leave, sometimes for extended periods.

While the Royal Navy sometimes used impressment – a form of seagoing conscription – most manpower needs were satisfied by volunters except during major wars, when the navy expanded to the largest size possible. Even in the opening stages of the American Revolutionary Wars most Royal Navy sailors were volunteers. It was only after French entry into the war that impressed sailors began to outnumber volunteers. In the revolutionary Continental Navy crews were all-volunteer, primarily because the Continental Navy had no means of enforcing conscription.

During this period men technically did not join the navy. Sailors joined ships. A sailor signed on to a ship's company for the length of a cruise. If the ship was a warship – whether of the Continental or the Royal Navy – the sailor was in the navy, but his enlistment lasted only as long as a ship was in commission. When the ship paid off at the end of the cruise – or the moment a ship was wrecked or captured in combat – that sailor became a free agent, outside the navy.

All navies tended to draw sailors from the same pool of mariners, regardless of nationality, especially since a sailor's allegiance then tended to lie with his ship rather than the nation of his birth. This was especially true of the Royal Navy and Continental Navy, which shared a common language, and for whom national allegiance tended to be due more to personal choice than to birth. Many born in Britain preferred to think of themselves as American, while many in the rebelling colonies chose fidelity to the Crown.

The Royal Dockyard at Deptford at the start of the American Revolution. Extensive shore facilities enabled the Royal Navy to keep its large fleet at sea. (LoC)

Sailors who showed aptitude in a required skill – carpentry, sail-making, navigation, or gunnery – could advance into the ranks of petty officers as a mate. A sailor who was skilled in shipboard carpentry could become a carpenter's mate, one with ability in shiphandling and navigation a master's mate, and those skilled in making and maintaining barrels could become cooper's mates. (The latter was a critical skill on a ship where food and water was stored in barrels.) Petty officers were appointed by a ship's commissioned officers.

The next step for an enlisted sailor was to become a warrant officer, who was in charge of some specialist aspect of the ship's operation. These included the ship's carpenter, cooper, and armorer, and the boatswain, in charge of the ship's rigging. The most senior warrant officer was the master – who was in charge of a ship's navigation, and treated with the dignity accorded a commissioned officer. Other warrant ranks included the surgeon, purser (responsible for a ship's finances), and chaplain. These warrants, along with the master, dined with the officers. The term "warrant rank" came from the warrants issued by the naval board to those holding these positions. In the Royal Navy, the senior warrants remained with a ship to look after it even when it was laid up out of commission.

Bonhomme Richard sailed from France with a crew of 187 seamen and boys, excluding the senior warrant officers. Of these, 43 were petty officers. *Serapis* carried a crew of 175 seamen and boys, and 52 petty officers – 227 in total.

An officer's commission marked him as a gentleman. Note the inked alterations in John Paul Jones's commission to designate him a naval, rather than an army officer. (MOA-UM)

In CONGRESS.

The DELEGATES of the UNITED STATES of *New Hampshire, Massachusetts Bay, Rhode-Island, Connecticut, New-York, New-Jersey, Pennsylvania, Delaware, Maryland, Virginia, North-Carolina, South-Carolina,* and *Georgia,* TO

John Paul Jones, Esquire,

WE, reposing especial Trust and Confidence in your Patriotism, Valour, Conduct, and Fidelity, DO, by these Presents, constitute and appoint you to be *Captain* ~~of the armed~~ ~~called the~~ ——————————— in the Service of the United States of North-America, fitted out for the Defence of American Liberty, and for repelling every hostile Invasion thereof. You are therefore carefully and diligently to discharge the Duty of *Captain* by doing and performing all manner of Things thereunto belonging. And we do strictly charge and require all Officers, Marines and Seamen under your Command, to be obedient to your Orders as *Captain* And you are to observe and follow such Orders and Directions from Time to Time as you shall receive from this or a future Congress of the United States, or Committee of Congress for that Purpose appointed, or Commander in Chief for the Time being of the Navy of the United States, or any other your superior Officer, according to the Rules and Discipline of War, the Usage of the Sea, and the Instructions herewith given you, in Pursuance of the Trust reposed in you. This Commission to continue in Force until revoked by this or a future Congress:

DATED at *Philadelphia October* 10th *1776.*

By Order of the CONGRESS,

John Hancock PRESIDENT.

ATTEST. *Cha Thomson secy*

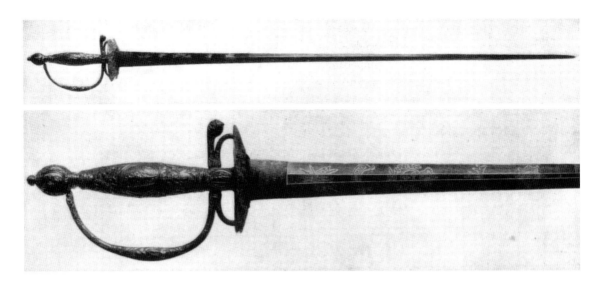

THE OFFICERS

Sword presented to John Paul Jones following the battle of Flamborough Head. Richard Pearson also received a presentation sword for the battle. (AC)

The ships of both the Continental and Royal Navies, including *Bonhomme Richard* and *Serapis*, were led by commissioned officers. These officers were responsible for directing a ship's operation and leading it in battle. These men held office through a commission issued to them by the government. In the Royal Navy, the commission was issued by the Board of the Admiralty, the governmental department that ran the Royal Navy. In the Continental Navy, it was issued by the Continental Congress. Both navies used a similar structure for their officer corps, and drew their officers from similar strata of society. At least in part, this was due to the Continental Congress drawing on the Royal Navy as an example when it created its navy.

The lowest-ranking officers aboard a warship, the midshipmen, were officer trainees. Both navies wanted capable officers, and created a flexible path to the quarterdeck. Royal Navy officers began as volunteers, typically at ages as young as 12 or 13. These boys were carried on the books as captain's servants, but spent their time learning the basics of seamanship, navigation, and leadership. Most of these candidates gained their appointments through influence – they or their parents knew someone commanding a King's ship, who gave them the position.

Midshipmen during this period were also drawn from promising members of a ship's crew as well as the gentry more usually associated with the Royal Navy officer corps. Competence was more valued than birth, as capable watch officers were critical to a ship's safety. A captain could sleep better with low-born but competent men running the watch, rather than incompetent relatives. In short, survival trumped nepotism, and as a result, the Royal Navy offered British society a degree of social mobility. In the Continental Navy, midshipmen were appointed by Congress, although captains could fill vacancies.

A midshipman who demonstrated competence could ascend the next step in the ladder of command – the rank of lieutenant, the lowest commissioned rank. In the

JOHN PAUL JONES

John Paul Jones was born on July 6, 1747, at Arbigland in Kirkcudbright, Scotland. He was born John Paul, Jr, the fourth child of seven. His father, John Paul, Sr (for whom he was named), was a gardener for William Craik, a local landowner. His mother, Jean MacDuff, was the daughter of a small farmer.

Despite humble beginnings, John Paul was ambitious, and he sought his fortune at sea. In 1761, aged 13, Paul signed articles of indenture as a ship's boy aboard *Friendship*, a 179-ton brig out of Whitehaven. *Friendship*'s owner retired in 1764, and released Paul from his indentures. With three years' seagoing experience, Paul signed on as third mate of *King George*, and then chief mate of *Two Friends*. Both were slave ships. The slave trade was then legal, and – due to high mortality rates – offered fast advancement.

Although Paul spent four years in what he later called the "abominable trade," he grew to despise it, leaving *Two Friends* at Kingston, Jamaica. Taking passage to Kirkcudbright on *John*, a 60-ton brig, Paul took command after both the captain and mate died en route, because Paul was the only one left aboard who could navigate.

He sailed *John* safely to Kirkcudbright, where the owners made Paul, then 21, captain. After two voyages commanding *John*, Paul moved to *Betsy*, a full-rigged ship, in 1772. In 1773 *Betsy* was in Barbados. During a wage dispute with his crew, John Paul killed a sailor. By his account, it was self-defense, but the man he killed was a local and popular. Paul fled, and disappeared for 20

John Paul Jones. (NHHC)

months. He re-emerged in Virginia in 1774, where his brother had lived. John Paul renamed himself John Paul Jones or John Jones, to protect himself from potential extradition to Barbados.

Royal Navy, a midshipman could not be commissioned until he had accumulated six years' service and had passed an examination before a board of captains. The Continental Navy lacked both requirements, with Congress issuing commissions based on personal recommendations from those believed knowledgeable – a process that occasionally misfired.

A two-decker had between three and five lieutenants. These men were responsible for running the ship. Lieutenants had to understand all aspects of a ship's operations – sail handling, seamanship, gunnery, and navigation – to do their job effectively. Good lieutenants could do these tasks as well as the seamen that normally did them.

He made sufficient contacts in Colonial society that with formation of the Continental Navy in December 1775, he was offered a lieutenant's commission as John Paul Jones. Accepting, he was appointed a lieutenant aboard *Alfred*, the 30-gun flagship of the Continental Navy's first squadron.

Jones soon established himself as both a competent and aggressive officer. He was given command of *Providence*, a 12-gun armed sloop, in May 1776. He remained on *Providence* for six months, capturing 16 British merchantmen during that period. Promoted to captain in August, he was given command of *Alfred* in October 1776. As a squadron commodore, he completed several successful two- and three-ship cruises. In July 1777 Jones took command of *Ranger*, a new, purpose-built 20-gun sloop-of-war. *Ranger* sailed to France in November 1777. There it received the first salute of an American flag by a foreign power. Jones concluded a successful Irish Sea cruise with *Ranger* in April 1778, which included raids at Whitehaven and St Mary's Island, and culminated in the capture of HMS *Drake* on April 24, 1778.

Jones then spent nearly a year ashore, without a command, despite being the most successful officer of the Continental Navy. Jones was offered *L'Indien*, a 40-gun frigate, but British diplomacy prevented Jones from taking possession of the ship. Instead, in June 1779 Jones agreed to captain *Bonhomme Richard*, and command a squadron of French and Continental warships. It took another two months before the squadron finally sailed on the war cruise envisioned by Jones, and in which he captured HMS *Serapis*, the largest British warship captured by the Continental Navy.

Jones played no further significant seagoing combat role in the Continental Navy. He took command of *Alliance*, a frigate present at Flamborough Head in November 1779, but *Alliance* was stolen by her previous captain in June 1780 and sailed back across the Atlantic. Left on French shores, Jones next took command of *Ariel*, a 26-gun frigate, but the ship was sent across the Atlantic *en flûte*, with nearly half of its guns stored below to make room for cargo.

Jones was then given command of *America*, a 74-gun ship-of-the-line then building in Portsmouth, New Hampshire. Jones's efforts resulted in the ship being completed shortly before the end of the American Revolutionary Wars – the only ship-of-the-line completed by the United States during the war. However, the ship was given to France at war's end.

Following the dissolution of the Continental Navy, Jones returned to Europe, seeking employment as a naval officer. Briefly a rear-admiral in the Russian Navy, he commanded the inshore squadron on the Black Sea in 1788. While he did a good job, he was dismissed by the Russians, largely due to complaints by British officers in Russian service. Jones then returned to Paris, then undergoing the French Revolution. Seeking employment, Jones died in Paris on July 18, 1792, shortly before a commission naming him as American consul to Algiers arrived.

An incompetent or lazy lieutenant could endanger a ship's safety, often by failing to recognize hazards or by ordering an improper action. This placed a premium on experience, and a ship's lieutenants were ranked by seniority, from the most senior (the first lieutenant) to the most junior (fourth or fifth lieutenant), based on the date of their commission.

One lieutenant, the watch officer, took charge of running the ship, acting for the ship's captain. In combat, the first lieutenant filled this role, but otherwise the junior lieutenants rotated as watch officer, taking the deck for four- or two-hour shifts. Crews were divided into two or three watches, which were further subdivided into divisions; each junior

lieutenant was responsible for one of these divisions, in charge of welfare and training for the men of his division. In addition, the first lieutenant was in charge of ship's discipline and supervised the more junior lieutenants.

In combat, the junior lieutenants commanded the guns, generally with one on each gun deck, while the first lieutenant acted as the captain's deputy. The most junior lieutenant was generally given responsibility for seeing that signals were sent properly, although if a ship were short of lieutenants, this task would be assigned a senior midshipman.

A lieutenant could also command a small warship – those mounting 22 or fewer guns. In that role, the lieutenant served as captain, and was called "captain" or "commander" (from lieutenant-commanding) while in this role. The modern ranks of commander and lieutenant-commander did not then exist, and these were courtesy titles.

The hazards of the sea, including storms, were a greater risk to a naval officer than combat. Self-preservation mitigated the risks inherent in influence, as competent officers helped reduced the chance of shipwreck, motivating captains to pick subordinates on the basis of ability. (AC)

Any ship larger than 24 guns was commanded by the next rank up the chain of command, that of full captain. To reach that rank, an officer had to distinguish himself in some way that marked him as superior to the other lieutenants. Distinguishing oneself in combat or an emergency was one way to do this. The first lieutenant of a warship winning a notable battle was often promoted to captain. Being the most competent lieutenant available when a vacancy for a captain existed was another way of achieving promotion to captain. Given the death rate in naval service, this offered frequent opportunities for promotion, although it required the favor of the admiral commanding the station.

Captains were in charge of all aspects of a ship and were responsible for everything that happened on or to his command. If a ship ran aground due to an incompetent watch officer or sleeping lookout, it was the captain's fault, even if the captain had been asleep in his cabin and delegated responsibility. The captain should have picked better men. As a result captains had extraordinary powers. They could order a man flogged or give the entire ship's crew leave. Most importantly, they commanded the ship in combat.

To be a successful officer required a man to be brave, intelligent, and physically capable. Navigation, one of the primary responsibilities of an officer, required the ability to master spherical trigonometry. The role also required physical bravery. In a boarding action, naval officers were expected to lead their men. While every promotion took an army officer further from danger, each promotion put an officer closer to danger. The junior lieutenants commanded the gun decks, sheltered by the bulwarks. The captain's and first lieutenant's station in combat was the most exposed and visible on the entire ship – on the quarterdeck, by the helm. Throw in the hazards posed by seagoing life – disease and shipwreck – and a naval officer of the 1700s had a 50 percent chance of dying violently during his service in the navy. Competence improved the chances, but luck helped.

A two-decker was a senior command, normally given to captains of demonstrated experience and seniority. In the Royal Navy, it was typically a post-captain's command – a post-captain being a full captain with at least three years' seniority. *Bonhomme Richard* was Jones's fourth command, and *Serapis* was the third ship that Pearson commanded. Including commissioned officers, senior warrants, and midshipmen, *Bonhomme Richard* had 20 officers aboard during its voyage. *Serapis* carried 23 commissioned officers, senior warrant officers, and midshipmen on its rolls.

THE MARINES

Naval combat of the era was fought at close quarters. As a result warships carried Marines to assist. *Bonhomme Richard* carried a large Marine contingent – 140 men; *Serapis* had 45 Marines aboard. In combat the Marines served as marksmen. They were stationed in a ship's fighting tops, the platforms where the top of the lower mast met the bottom of the topmast, or along a ship's bulwarks, particularly along the quarterdeck.

In close combat, Marines fought hand-to-hand, either to defend their ship, or take the enemy's. Marines formed the core of the boarding parties, and any landing parties, if a ship's crew were committed to an action on land. They handled lines on the deck, and worked the great guns, but were not used aloft to handle the sails. Marines also provided shipboard security, and were used to maintain shipboard discipline. Marine sentries guarded the magazines, arms, and spirit room. Marines were posted at hatches during battle to prevent sailors from seeking refuge in the hold.

Marines were drawn from a different pool of men than sailors, and enlisted in a unit rather than on a ship. Some rivalry between Marines and sailors was fostered by ships' officers, as one function of the Marines was to put down mutiny, and it was feared that if the two groups became too friendly, they may be unwilling to. Marines messed and slept between the officers (who lived aft) and the sailors (who were berthed forward) to provide distance between officers and the crew. The Marines, as soldiers, wore uniforms, while sailors of the era did not.

As a Continental warship *Bonhomme Richard*'s Marines should have come from the United States Marine Corps, a Continental unit modeled on the Royal Navy's Marine Regiment, but in France, where *Bonhomme Richard* was outfitted, Jones would have had

Sailors eating a meal aboard a warship. While life as a warship sailor was hard, sailors ate better than common laborers ashore. (LoC)

RICHARD PEARSON

Richard Pearson came from the landed gentry that formed the backbone of the Royal Navy's officer corps in the 18th century. Born in March 1731, at Lanton Hall near Appleby in Westmoreland, he entered the navy in 1745 aboard HMS *Dover*, a 44-gun two-decker. He soon transferred to HMS *Seaford*, a 24-gun sixth-rate sloop-of-war, commanded by Captain John Willson, a kinsman. Pearson joined the ship in the Mediterranean, where it spent three years during the War of the Austrian Succession (1740–48).

In 1749 Pearson secured a midshipman's posting on HMS *Amazon*, a 26-gun cruiser commanded by Captain Arthur Gardiner. Peacetime service offered little opportunity for advancement, and Willson (likely Pearson's patron) died in 1749, reducing Mr Midshipman Pearson's Royal Navy influence. Pearson left the navy, taking service with the Honourable East India Company in 1750.

He returned to the Royal Navy in 1755, when North American events threatened a war between Britain and France. Pearson passed his lieutenant's examination on November 5, and was appointed fourth lieutenant of *Elizabeth*, a 64-gun ship-of-the-line. *Elizabeth* spent 1756 on blockade duty off France, patrolling the Bay of Biscay.

In 1757 *Elizabeth* went to the East Indies under Charles Steevens. While in the Indies, the ship participated in three major naval battles: Cuddalore (April 29, 1758), Negapatam (August 3, 1758), and Pondicherry (September 10, 1759). Pearson was

Sir Richard Pearson. (AC)

badly wounded in battle, but distinguished himself. When Steevens was promoted to rear-admiral, he had Pearson appointed first lieutenant of his flagship, the 74-gun *Norfolk*.

Norfolk's captain, Richard Kempenfelt, soon shared Steeven's high opinion of Pearson. Pearson temporarily took command of *Norfolk* in the midst of a violent

trouble recruiting enough individuals to satisfy his desire for Marines. He wanted an oversized Marine contingent because he hoped to make landings on England, and wanted extra men to man prizes.

Jones turned to his French allies for help, and they provided the ship's Marine contingent. While France had its own *Corps-Royal d'Infanterie de Marine* (Royal Marine Corps), these men were needed by the French Navy. Instead France gave *Bonhomme Richard* a Marine contingent from the red-coated *Régiment de Walsh-Sérrant*. One of three regiments of Irish infantry then serving the French Crown, it was a logical choice as many of its men spoke English.

cyclone on January 1, 1861. Kempenfelt was disabled in an accident and Pearson saw *Norfolk* safely through the storm. This should have gained Pearson command of the 60-gun *Tiger* as a reward, which would have given Pearson "post rank" as a full captain. Steevens had made out the commission, but died before it was signed. Pearson was passed over by the new admiral, instead serving as first lieutenant of the 74-gun *Lennox* at the siege of Manila in September 1762. Pearson returned to England in 1763, remaining on half-pay until 1769.

In 1769 Pearson was appointed first lieutenant of the 60-gun *Dunkirk*, which was sent to Jamaica. As before, Pearson impressed his captain, Arthur Forrest, and promised command of the first vacancy. Temporarily given command of *Phoenix*, a 44-gun two-decker, in August 1770, Pearson was denied the post when his patron again died before command was confirmed. Instead the Admiralty appointed him to *Druid*, a ten-gun sloop, with a commander's commission. He commanded *Druid* from October 1771 to 1773 when he transferred to command of *Speedwell*, a ketch-rigged 18-gun sloop-of-war. On June 25, with *Speedwell* at a royal review at Spithead, Pearson was promoted to post rank in a special promotion.

In 1776, Pearson finally received a post-captain's command – the 24-gun *Garland*. *Garland* and Pearson escorted a convoy to Quebec. After arriving in North America, *Garland* patrolled the waters around the St Lawrence for the next two years.

In 1778 Pearson returned to Britain, where he took command of a 44-gun two-decker then under construction, *Serapis*. Commissioned in May 1779, *Serapis* served in home waters, escorting Baltic convoys. While escorting a convoy, *Serapis* met Jones's squadron off Flamborough Head, and fought the action described in this book.

Pearson's career after the battle of Flamborough Head was anticlimactic. He took command of the 32-gun *Alarm* in January 1780, but it was a dockyard command while the frigate went through a refit, pending his court-martial for the loss of *Serapis*. He was honorably acquitted at that trial on March 10, 1780. Afterwards he was made captain of the 38-gun frigate *Arethusa*, a command he held for the rest of the war until the frigate paid off in January 1783. During this period he fought at the second battle of Ushant and served in North American waters.

Despite the defeat, Pearson was hailed as a hero in Britain, for preserving the convoy. He was granted the freedom of the towns of Hull, Scarborough, Lancaster, and Appleby, and awarded silver plates by the Russia Company and the Royal Exchange Assurance Company. Ultimately, he was knighted for his defense of the convoy on April 30, 1780.

In 1790 he retired to the Royal Naval Hospital, Greenwich. In 1800 he became lieutenant-governor of Greenwich Hospital upon the death of the previous lieutenant-governor. He served in that role until his death on January 26, 1806.

Serapis carried the standard Marine contingent for a Royal Navy 44-gun two-decker. These men would have been assigned from the Royal Navy's Marine regiment (it would not become the Royal Marines until 1802). At full strength, *Serapis*'s Marine detachment would have one lieutenant, one sergeant, two corporals, a drummer, and 40 men. While significantly smaller than its opponent's Marine detachment, these sea soldiers were among the best Marines around.

COMBAT

John Paul Jones' greatest desire was a warship to command in combat. "I wish to have no connection with any ship that does not sail fast," he once wrote in a letter to Le Ray de Chaumont, an advisor to the French king, "For I intend to go in harm's way." In April 1778, he took the sloop-of-war *Ranger* on a successful cruise in the Irish Sea that created an uproar in Britain. Since returning to France in early May of that year Jones had been seeking a new opportunity to strike Britain. He was the most renowned naval officer of the Continental Navy, but by November 1778 he was still unemployed.

It was not for lack of trying. He had been offered *L'Indien*, a 40-gun frigate. Being built in the Netherlands, it was a true frigate, a design based on the large 38-gun 18-pounder frigates with which Britain and France had begun experimenting. The British got wind of this, and used diplomacy to prevent its release to any belligerents – not just the United States, but also France. Several other potential commands, prizes taken from Britain, were retained by the French Navy, even though the French Crown had promised Jones something. Offered command of a French privateer by de Chaumont, Jones refused – he was an American naval officer, not a foreign privateer. Finally, in November, a ship was found – *Duc de Duras*.

It was hardly the fast ship that Jones desired. *Duc de Duras* was elderly and weary. A French East Indiaman, the ship was laid up at L'Orient, France's port for the East Indies trade. It would require a complete refit – and required conversion into a warship. But it was a ship of force. At 990 tons it would be the largest warship in the United States Navy. Jones believed it a white elephant, but like true white elephants, once it was offered the gift had to be accepted. *Duc de Duras* was renamed *Bonhomme Richard* to honor Benjamin Franklin, taking the name from the pseudonymous author of Franklin's *Poor Richard's Almanac*. Jones set about outfitting the ship for sea, a process that would take six months.

At about the same time in Britain, Richard Pearson was going through the same labors as Jones, but enjoying it a great deal more. Pearson had been given command of *Serapis*, a 44-gun fifth-rate two-decker just out of the builder's yard. For Pearson, outfitting the new ship was a reward for 30 years' loyal and able service as a Royal Navy officer. It was not quite the 60-gun *Tiger* snatched from him 16 years earlier, but this command was real, and brand new.

By June 1779, *Bonhomme Richard* was ready for sea. *Serapis* was already in commission, and getting ready for its first assignment – escorting a convoy to the Baltic and back. *Bonhomme Richard* would remain in port for another month, preparing for its upcoming assignment as the flagship of an American squadron. This time Jones planned to take his squadron around Ireland and Great Britain, raiding British ports, and capturing a British ship along the way. His goal was to force the Royal Navy to redeploy ships from North American to European waters.

Pierre Landais, a French naval officer, held a captain's commission in the Continental Navy. Today many naval historians believe him to have been insane. He was eventually relieved of duty due to his bizarre behavior. It was Jones's misfortune to have Landais commanding *Alliance* at the battle of Flamborough Head. (AC)

THE CRUISE BEGINS

The squadron, consisting of seven ships, set sail on August 14. In addition to *Bonhomme Richard*, it contained *Alliance*, *Pallas*, *Vengeance*, and two privateers, *Monsieur* and *Granville*. *Alliance* was a 38-gun Continental Navy frigate, newly arrived from the United States. It was commanded by Captain Pierre Landais, a French naval officer serving in the Continental Navy. *Pallas* was a 32-gun frigate with a 9-pounder main battery, and *Vengeance* a 12-gun brig. Both were on loan from the French Navy, with French crews and officers, but flying the American flag. The two privateers were also French, sailing under French letters-of-marque. Free operators, they chose to accompany the squadron because it was convenient.

The expedition proved – in the words of naval historian Samuel Elliot Morrison – to be "a mad cruise." *Monsieur* and *Granville* left the squadron before it reached the Irish coast eight days later. Their captains learned that the commodore was serious about seeking out warships and landing raiding parties on shore – activities counterproductive to privateers' profit. Additionally, *Alliance*, *Pallas*, and *Vengeance* left and rejoined the squadron virtually at will.

While Jones's appearance off southwest Ireland caused a stir, he failed to find any British warships to fight. Once they learned Jones was at sea, the Royal Navy sent its available naval resources to the Irish Sea, where they assumed Jones was heading.

Captain Richard Pearson
interposed his escorting
warships between Jones's
squadron and his convoy to
give the merchant ships time
to reach the safety of
Scarborough Bay (shown here
as it appeared in 1898),
where they would be
sheltered by the guns of
Scarborough Castle. (LoC)

Meanwhile, Jones's squadron sailed north around Scotland, reaching the Orkney Islands by September 3. But other than taking a number of merchantmen as prizes it had accomplished little.

The prizes were sent to Bergen in Norway – against Jones's orders – by Landais, who then disappeared, with *Alliance*. Jones next attempted to land at Leith in the Firth of Forth and hold it to ransom, and then raid Newcastle-upon-Tyne to disrupt coal shipments from that point. Contrary winds frustrated the first attempt, and unwilling captains prevented the second. They would not support a landing, and *Bonhomme Richard* lacked the manpower to attempt the raid alone. Jones turned his squadron south.

Following the Yorkshire coast south from Newcastle he hoped to capture more colliers. He took a collier and a sloop off Whitby, and, off Scarborough on September 22, a second collier and an English-flagged brigantine returning from Rotterdam. He pressed *Bonhomme Richard* south of the Humber River, seeking more prizes, but only took two small pilot schooners, one of which was taken when it sailed up to the captured brigantine. He took the pilots aboard *Bonhomme Richard*, and put prize crews aboard the pilot boats, intending to use them as scouts.

By this time the squadron had scattered, with *Pallas* seeking prizes off Scarborough. When the wind shifted to the north-northwest, Jones turned *Bonhomme Richard* north, to find his consorts. He found them shortly after midnight, but was unable to identify them until the dawn. Then he saw that not only was *Pallas* there, but so was *Alliance*, which had disappeared two weeks earlier. The squadron continued north under very light winds, when at 2.00pm on September 23 one of the two schooners reported many sail to the north, off Flamborough Head.

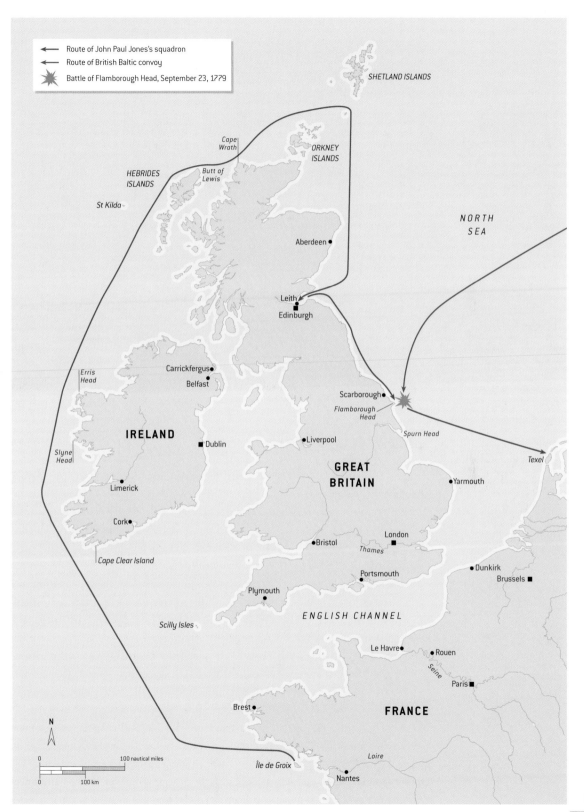

Route of John Paul Jones's squadron
Route of British Baltic convoy
Battle of Flamborough Head, September 23, 1779

SHETLAND ISLANDS

Cape Wrath

ORKNEY ISLANDS

HEBRIDES ISLANDS

Butt of Lewis

St Kilda

NORTH SEA

Aberdeen

Leith

Edinburgh

Erris Head

Carrickfergus

Belfast

Scarborough

Flamborough Head

Slyne Head

IRELAND

Dublin

Liverpool

Spurn Head

Texel

GREAT BRITAIN

Limerick

Yarmouth

Cork

London

Cape Clear Island

Bristol

Thames

Dunkirk

Brussels

Portsmouth

Plymouth

Le Havre

Rouen

ENGLISH CHANNEL

Scilly Isles

Seine

Paris

Brest

FRANCE

N

0   100 nautical miles

0   100 km

Loire

Île de Groix

Nantes

OPENING STAGES

It was a British convoy, 41 merchant ships carrying cargoes from the Baltic. Shepherding it were two escorts – the 44-gun two-decker *Serapis*, commanded by Richard Pearson, and the 20-gun sloop-of-war *Countess of Scarborough*, commanded by Thomas Piercy, a lieutenant-commanding. It was the type of opportunity that Jones had been seeking during the whole cruise. Destroying the convoy would hurt Britain badly.

Pearson, in overall command of the convoy, was aware that an enemy squadron was in the vicinity. Jones's passage along the Yorkshire coast had raised the alarm throughout the county. The local militia had been turned out, shore batteries manned, and warnings sent to the Admiralty in London. Scarborough Castle was flying a large red flag, a signal for "enemy on our shores." The signal was spotted by the convoy, slowly moving south against contrary winds, as it passed Scarborough. Pearson took *Serapis* into Scarborough Bay, where at 10.00am he was approached by a fishing boat, sent by town officials warning of the Continental squadron to the south.

Pearson immediately stood out of Scarborough Bay. He fired a signal gun to attract the convoy's attention, and hoisted the signal for the convoy to remain upwind of *Serapis*. While some ships followed his orders, many ignored it, continuing south for London and home. By early afternoon, the convoy's leading ships spotted unknown warships to the south – Jones's squadron. Finally aware that there was more to their convoy commander's signaling than an attempt to annoy them, these ships slowed, and let their topgallant sails fly – a signal for "strange sails in sight."

At 1.00pm masthead lookouts on *Serapis*, chasing its wayward convoy, also spotted the Continental squadron. Pearson ordered the convoy to sail to the northwest, and head for the shelter offered by the heavy guns of Scarborough Castle. It was a command enthusiastically, if not necessarily efficiently, obeyed by the various masters of the merchant ships. The convoy dissolved into disorder as the captains frantically turned their ships about to head for safety. By 4.00pm, as they headed north, Pearson could see the enemy ships from his quarterdeck. He counted four, at least one of which appeared to be a 64-gun ship or an Indiaman, and two of which seemed to be frigates. Although badly outnumbered on paper, Pearson was undeterred. He ordered *Countess of Scarborough* to fall in behind him and moved against the enemy warships.

To the south, Jones was attempting to organize his squadron. Wind favored him, as it was blowing to the north, but it was only a breeze and the afternoon current, on the flood, was against him. *Bonhomme Richard* crawled under such conditions, even though Jones had all sail set, including studding sails on his topsails. By 3.00pm he could see the enemy ships, and at 3.30pm he fired a gun to recall the pilot boat, and hoisted signal "General Chase," directing his ships to engage the enemy.

The two groups of ships were closing at the pace of two walking men. Both sides intended to fight. Pearson was determined to defend his convoy; Jones was determined to beat an English warship; Landais, aboard *Alliance*, was determined to do mischief; and the remaining captains determined to do their duties as they saw fit. The slow, deliberate approach gave both sides time to prepare for battle. All the ships cleared for action between 4.00pm and 6.00pm. Unnecessary items from the gun decks were stored below. Magazines were unlocked, and the guns loaded and manned. Small arms were distributed and men sent to quarters. Ships went to battle sail, clewing up their courses and furling unnecessary sails.

Sunset was at 6.00pm. As the sun touched the horizon, Jones gave the signal for his squadron to form a line of battle. The signal was ignored. *Alliance* sailed ahead of *Bonhomme Richard*. *Pallas*, off to one side, continued a northward course while Jones ordered *Bonhomme Richard* to the northwest to parallel *Serapis*. *Vengeance* chose to watch events unfold. The pilot schooner, with 15 men and a lieutenant from *Bonhomme Richard* aboard, had missed the signal to rejoin and was hopelessly astern. Instead of fighting a coordinated squadron action, Jones had to settle for a series of single-ship duels, outside his control. He still had command of *Bonhomme Richard*, and intended to fight with it alone, if necessary. He continued closing on *Serapis*.

Meanwhile, Pearson, on *Serapis*, was equally determined to fight – and perhaps relieved to see that he would only be engaging the enemy two-decker. He could see the frigates move away from their flagship. Upwind of *Bonhomme Richard*, Pearson had been sailing southeast in an attempt to gain the weather gage – the upwind position. At 6.00pm, seeing the still-unknown ship turn from north-northeast to a northwest course, Pearson tacked *Serapis* to keep his ship between the convoy and the enemy. Turning into the wind *Serapis* ended on an almost due west track, converging on *Bonhomme Richard*. Pearson ordered the red ensign hoisted and as

This model of a warship's lower gun deck illustrates the conditions found there. It was cramped, and in battle it was noisy and smoke-filled. Even in daylight it was dark. During a nighttime battle it was easy for unused gunpowder cartridges to become forgotten and accumulate in dark corners. (AC-HMM)

a symbol of defiance, nailed the flag to the staff, to let his crew know that *Serapis* would never strike her colors.

For the next hour, in the gathering darkness, the two ships closed. In an attempt to draw *Serapis* close, where Jones could use the advantage he had in Marine marksmen, Jones had *Bonhomme Richard* fly a British ensign. This was a legitimate ploy, as long as a ship did not fire until its own ensign was flying. By 7.15pm, under a clear night lit by a full moon, the two ships were within hailing distance, 100yd apart.

Pearson called across, "This is His Majesty's Ship *Serapis*. What ship is that?" Still flying the British ensign, Jones had *Bonhomme Richard*'s master reply, "The *Princess Royal*." There was an Indiaman of that name, but Pearson was not fooled. He demanded "Where from?" Hearing no response, he hailed, "Answer immediately or I shall be forced to fire upon you." Jones immediately answered by lowering the British ensign, and hoisting the Stars and Stripes. Pearson responded by opening *Serapis*'s

The new United States flag flew over *Bonhomme Richard* and *Alliance* at Flamborough Head. However, since the instructions sent to France were unclear, the two ships flew different versions of the Stars and Stripes:
left – *Alliance*,
right – *Bonhomme Richard*.
(USN)

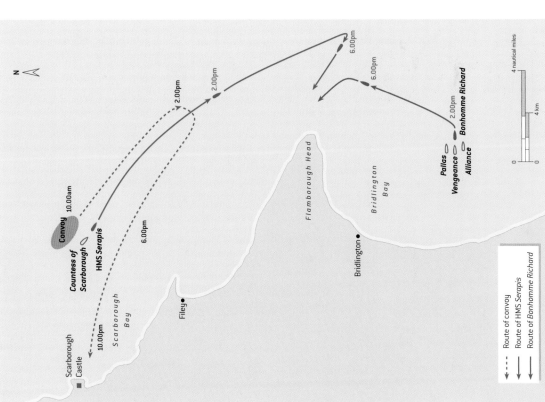

Key Events

1. 5:00pm: both ships clear for action.
2. 6:00pm: *Serapis* tacks to cut off *Bonhomme Richard* from the Baltic convoy under Pearson's charge.
3. 7:00pm: the two ships maneuver broadside to broadside.
4. 7:20pm: both ships open fire.
5. 7:30pm: *Serapis* crosses *Bonhomme Richard*'s stern, and rakes *Bonhomme Richard*.
6. *Serapis* crosses *Bonhomme Richard*'s bow, and rakes *Bonhomme Richard*.
7. *Serapis* attempts to cross *Bonhomme Richard*'s bow, luffs up and *Bonhomme Richard* runs into *Serapis*'s quarter.
8. *Bonhomme Richard* backs clear of *Serapis*.
9. *Bonhomme Richard* fouls *Serapis* in an attempt to fore*Serapis*.
10. 8:00pm: *Bonhomme Richard* fouls *Serapis* while crossing *Serapis*'s bow.
11. 8:15pm: The two ships lock together from the collision. Pearson attempts to free *Serapis* while Jones orders the two ships lashed together.
12. 8:30pm: *Serapis* drops its port anchor in an attempt to free the ship from *Bonhomme Richard*.
13. The two ships drift broadside to broadside, as Jones has more grapples thrown to connect the two ships.
14. Pearson is unable to free *Serapis* and the battle continues with both ships trading broadsides and musket fire.
15. 10:00pm: *Alliance* sails into battle, firing into both ships, but mainly into *Bonhomme Richard*. Pearson, unaware that *Alliance* is hitting *Bonhomme Richard*, surrenders *Serapis*.

Legend

Path of HMS *Serapis*
HMS *Serapis* drifting
Path of *Bonhomme Richard*
Bonhomme Richard drifting

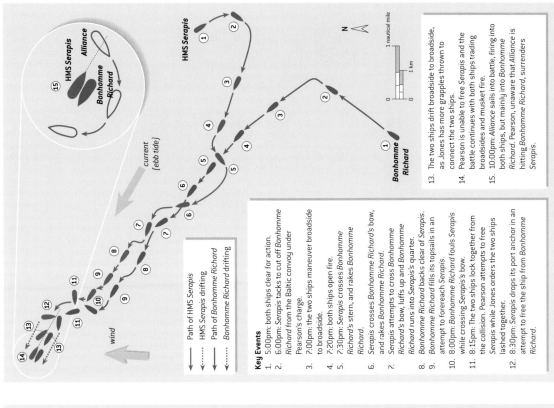

gunports, and running out the guns. The ships were now within pistol shot – separated by perhaps 25yd. As the American ensign reached the top of the staff, both ships simultaneously fired a broadside. The battle was on.

THE BATTLE COMMENCES

The first broadside in a battle is critical. It is generally the only broadside in which there is time to carefully load and aim the guns. After that first round, fired on the order of the ship's captain, gun crews fired independently, emphasizing speed, and trying to achieve a maximum rate of fire. Additionally, in a battle like this, where both sides intended to close to the minimum possible range before firing, that first broadside would have been double-shotted. Each gun would have been loaded with two round-shot instead of one, effectively doubling the weight of metal thrown by each gun.

Double-shotting held risks. It took extra time to double-shot a gun, reducing the critical rate of fire. It involved more strain on firing, which could upset the gun off its carriage. There was also a risk that the gun would burst, although that usually only happened later in a battle, when the guns were hot, the heat weakening the gun as the metal softened.

It is not known if Pearson ordered *Serapis*'s guns double-shotted on that first broadside. It was not mentioned in his post-battle reports. It is known that Pearson aimed low, at his opponent's hull, on that critical first broadside. Not only was that standard British tactics, but the first broadside in fact slammed into *Bonhomme Richard*'s hull. So it was likely double-shotted, especially as loading time was not a consideration on the first broadside.

On *Bonhomme Richard*, only its lower-deck 18-pounders were double-shotted, and loaded with round shot. Jones had ordered the rest of the guns to be loaded with double-headed shot – a form of ammunition intended to knock down masts and rigging, typically two disks linked with chain or a metal bar. Additionally, these guns were fired high – at the sails and masts, rather than at the hull. Jones felt that he had to neutralize *Serapis*'s speed advantage to win the battle.

The results were predictable. *Serapis*'s first broadside cut through *Bonhomme Richard*, while most of *Bonhomme Richard*'s cut through air. The two ships then traded a second set of broadsides – this time at 20yd – first *Serapis*, then *Bonhomme Richard*. The results of this exchange were even more devastating to *Bonhomme Richard* than the first – with much of the damage done by *Bonhomme Richard*'s own guns.

At least one of *Bonhomme Richard*'s three double-shotted lower-deck guns burst on that second broadside. The explosion killed or wounded most of the 60 men manning the battery. Two of the three 18-pounders on the engaged starboard side were dismounted. A hole was blown in the ship's side and the deck above damaged. Jones ordered the lower-deck guns abandoned. Survivors were sent to man the upper-deck guns.

Jones's bad beginning to the battle was to get worse. The ships were so close that *Bonhomme Richard*, with its loftier rig, blanketed *Serapis*, literally taking the wind

from *Serapis*'s sails. *Serapis* fell behind *Bonhomme Richard*. This gave Jones an opportunity to cross *Serapis*'s bow and fire a crippling broadside down the length of the ship, but *Bonhomme Richard* took too long to turn. Instead, once aft of *Bonhomme Richard*, with the wind again filling its sails, *Serapis* crossed *Bonhomme Richard*'s stern and fired three quick raking broadsides into *Bonhomme Richard*'s exposed stern.

The results were devastating. These broadsides were fired by *Serapis*'s previously disengaged starboard battery, including the carefully loaded first broadside. Ripping through the windows of the stern gallery, the shots tore down the length of the ship, scything down anyone or anything in its path. Most of the Marines on the poop were killed or wounded as were nearly half of *Bonhomme Richard*'s upper-deck gun crews.

Serapis then sailed up *Bonhomme Richard*'s port side, firing another broadside into *Bonhomme Richard*'s flank. *Bonhomme Richard* responded, but its broadside was feeble – ragged and disorganized, as gun crews took time to pull themselves together from the effects of the raking broadsides. The battle was less than 15 minutes old, and Jones was losing, and losing badly.

Pearson now took the faster, copper-bottomed *Serapis* across *Bonhomme Richard*'s bow. Due to the vagaries of the wind, *Serapis* crossed *Bonhomme Richard*'s bow at an oblique angle, and could not fire. *Bonhomme Richard*'s bowsprit hit *Serapis*, thrusting

QUARTERDECK VIEW – *SERAPIS*

Richard Pearson stands on his quarterdeck in the opening stages of the battle. He has stern-raked *Bonhomme Richard*, and fired several devastating broadsides into her sides as well. The enemy ship's fire has been largely ineffective, mostly flying over *Serapis*. Even though fluky winds prevent *Serapis* from again raking *Bonhomme Richard* as *Serapis* passes across the Indiaman's bow, Pearson has to feel satisfied. His enemy is badly damaged. *Serapis*'s superior maneuverability and firepower will settle the outcome.

To Pearson, his opponent's situation appears to be hopeless. The Yankee warship cannot gain victory through the firepower of the privateer's guns, and lacks the speed to run away from *Serapis*. Its consorts cannot offer assistance, as they have either run or engaged with other ships. A reasonable opponent would recognize this, and wish to avoid unnecessary bloodshed.

Neither ship can fire at the other, creating a rare moment of silence during the battle. Pearson can see his opposite number on the quarterdeck of the rebel privateer, a short, restless man. Mistaking the short man's frustration for anxiety, Pearson decides to offer his opponent quarter, shouting across to the opposing captain. "Do you strike?"

But Pearson receives an unexpected answer.

QUARTERDECK VIEW – *BONHOMME RICHARD*

"I have not yet begun to fight!"

The declaration is one of the touchstones of the story of John Paul Jones, a part of his legend. Yet controversy surrounds the remark. Did John Paul Jones really say it? The record of the statement comes from Richard Dale. While Dale was first lieutenant of *Bonhomme Richard*, he was in charge of the 12-pounder battery, one deck below the quarterdeck where Jones stood. Dale also first related the story 46 years after the battle, during retirement after a distinguished career in the United States Navy. Besides, why would Jones have said he was just beginning to fight three hours into the battle?

If Jones did say those words – or something similar – he probably uttered them early in the battle. Pearson did call on the Continental warship to surrender shortly after the battle began, when *Serapis* crossed *Bonhomme Richard*'s bow, as shown here, from the point of view of Jones, on *Bonhomme Richard*'s quarterdeck. Since neither ship's guns could to brought to bear, it would have been relatively quiet. Dale, standing in the waist between the two captains, could clearly have heard both challenge and response. And Jones always had a way with a turn of a phrase and healthy lungs with which to make an audible – and appropriate – answer.

John Paul Jones shown shooting a sailor during the battle of Flamborough Head. The incident did not happen. Although Jones did call for two sailors attempting to surrender *Bonhomme Richard* to be shot, these men were clubbed down and not shot. The story arose as part of a yarn told by a British member of *Bonhomme Richard*'s crew who deserted to Yorkshire the day after the battle. (LoC)

over its quarter galleries. But Pearson could look down the length of *Bonhomme Richard*'s deck and see a ship that appeared beaten. He hailed his opposite number, whose identity was probably unknown, and called out, "Do you strike?"

It was a logical question, but it was not a question Jones was in the mood to answer affirmatively. Instead he gave an emphatic refusal. According to Richard Dale, *Bonhomme Richard*'s first lieutenant, who would have been near Jones, Jones replied with the now-immortal "I have not yet begun to fight!" Others claim Jones said something else, but in a similar vein. Regardless, Jones let Pearson know that the fight would continue.

Now the two ships began paralleling each other, sailing northwest. By now Jones realized that he could not win a gunnery duel, and that the copper-bottomed *Serapis* could outsail *Bonhomme Richard* in the light wind they were experiencing. Jones's attempts to disable *Serapis*'s sails had failed. His one chance for victory was to lay alongside *Serapis*, where the Continental advantage in numbers of Marines would count.

His first attempt failed. Jones ordered *Bonhomme Richard*'s helm put over and attempted to reach *Serapis*. Pearson saw what Jones was doing and danced ahead of *Bonhomme Richard*. Jones saw that *Bonhomme Richard* going to pass astern of *Serapis*. While this offered an opportunity to stern-rake *Serapis*, Jones knew one broadside from *Bonhomme Richard* was unlikely to disable *Serapis*. Once *Bonhomme Richard* passed *Serapis*, it would be downwind of *Serapis*, giving *Serapis* the wind gage, and the ability to choose the distance at which the two ships fought, making it impossible for *Bonhomme Richard* to reach *Serapis* in near-calm winds. Jones bore to larboard to await another opportunity.

It came a few minutes later. An odd puff of wind that reached *Bonhomme Richard*, but not *Serapis*, allowed Jones to draw ahead. He then cut across *Serapis*'s bow. The wind died, and instead of *Bonhomme Richard* crossing ahead of *Serapis*, the two ships collided. As *Bonhomme Richard* slid across *Serapis*'s bow, *Serapis*'s bowsprit locked into *Bonhomme Richard*'s poop. It was 8.00pm and the battle was 45 minutes old.

GRAPPLED

Jones immediately saw the opportunity that was being offered. He had his men grapple the two ships together. Grappling irons – multi-pronged iron hooks that look like a four-pronged fishhook – were tossed across to *Serapis*. Ropes were tied to eyes in the base of these hooks. As the irons hooked into *Serapis*'s rigging and bulwark rails, Continental sailors lashed the other end of the ropes to *Bonhomme Richard*. As many as 50 lines were tossed across. *Serapis* was becoming tied to *Bonhomme Richard* by a spider's web of lines.

Pearson saw the danger in forfeiting *Serapis*'s advantage of mobility. He ordered the grapples cast off, to free *Serapis* from *Bonhomme Richard*'s embrace. But as his sailors attempted to do this, they were shot down. Jones had placed a large contingent of sharpshooters in *Bonhomme Richard*'s fighting tops – perhaps twice what *Serapis* would have had stationed in her tops. Well above *Bonhomme Richard*'s decks, the men in her fighting tops had been spared the effects of *Serapis*'s guns.

These sailors initially concentrated on their opposite numbers aboard *Serapis*. By this point in the battle, their superior numbers had cleared *Serapis*'s fighting tops, allowing the marksmen on *Bonhomme Richard* to turn their attention to the men on deck. Any British sailor reaching for a grappling iron would have been exposed to their fire, and an easy target.

The two ships were soon drifting together, rotating from the oblique angle of initial contact until they were broadside to broadside, pointing in opposite directions. As the angle closed, and seeing that his men could not free *Serapis* from *Bonhomme Richard*'s grappling hooks, Pearson ordered *Serapis*'s larboard anchor dropped. He hoped the shock of the anchor gripping home would snap the thin grapple lines, but the attempt failed. The two ships were inescapably linked, held in place by *Serapis*'s anchor.

Serapis's superior battery quickly silenced *Bonhomme Richard*'s gun decks. Soon only *Bonhomme Richard*'s quarterdeck 8-pounders were still firing, pointed personally by Jones. Meanwhile *Serapis*'s 18-pounders ripped huge holes in *Bonhomme Richard*'s lower deck, while the British 9-pounders tore apart the upper deck. Despite this, the struggle was now more even. Jones had ordered his surviving crew into *Bonhomme Richard*'s upper works as marksmen. They had abandoned the great guns, and were using

---

OVERLEAF

William Hamilton and the grenade toss

The grenades carried aboard *Bonhomme Richard* were hollow iron balls about the size and shape of a large pomegranate (from which the name originated), filled with gunpowder, and fitted with a six-second fuse. Grenades were ignited by slow-match, a slowly burning cloth wick normally used to touch off the guns. Unless dropped from above, grenades could be as dangerous to the user as they were to the target. Using them aloft was awkward, as a sailor needed one hand for the grenade, one hand for the match, and one hand to hang onto the rigging, so they were used infrequently.

William Hamilton, a Scots seaman aboard *Bonhomme Richard*, saw the opportunity to use grenades, and found a way to use them aloft. He carried the grenades aloft in a canvas bag, and probably held the lit slow-match in his teeth, allowing him to use both hands as he crawled out on to the mainyard. Once in position, he could hang onto the yard with an arm and both legs, grab a grenade from his bag, light it, and toss it on to *Serapis*. And – as shown here – get lucky enough to bounce one on to *Serapis*'s lower gun deck, where it would touch off 6lb gunpowder cartridges left on deck.

muskets fired from the forecastle, quarterdeck, poop, and fighting tops to cut down *Serapis*'s crew.

Just as *Bonhomme Richard*'s crew abandoned the gun decks, *Serapis*'s abandoned the upper decks. Pearson ordered his crew to shelter, off the exposed waist, quarterdeck, and forecastle. Only Pearson and a small party of messengers and Marines remained on deck to keep an eye on Continental attempts to board. By now, fires were raging on both ships. *Serapis*'s gunfire had touched off its own rigging and sails, and started fires on *Bonhomme Richard*'s gun decks.

For the first three hours of the fight the battle had remained a single-ship action. *Pallas* had squared off against the smaller *Countess of Scarborough*, which it eventually captured. Too small to engage the British warships, *Vengeance* sat out the fight. *Alliance* had hared off in the darkness. At 9.20pm, *Alliance* entered the fight, sailing slowly under topsails to the two motionless combatants. As the frigate passed *Bonhomme Richard*'s stern *Alliance* fired a raking broadside, striking both ships.

Near the end of the battle, Pearson led an attempt to board *Bonhomme Richard*, but superior numbers of Continental sailors and marines repulsed the attempt. (NARA)

Men from *Bonhomme Richard* called out to *Alliance*, shouting that she had fired on the wrong ship. Night signals were made on *Bonhomme Richard* to identify the ex-Indiaman as a friend. Despite shouts from *Bonhomme Richard* for *Alliance* to lay alongside *Serapis* and board, *Alliance* continued its course – and fired a second broadside. This one smashed through *Bonhomme Richard*'s stern. Once past, the Continental frigate wore around, and crossed the bow of *Bonhomme Richard*, firing a third and final broadside at 10.00pm, most of which struck *Bonhomme Richard*. It then sailed back into the darkness to take no further action in the battle.

Landais's actions were almost certainly deliberate. Given a full moon and the illumination from fires on both ships, Landais could hardly have mistaken the distinctive silhouette of *Bonhomme Richard* for a British warship. After the battle, he confided to a French officer that he wanted *Bonhomme Richard* to sink, so that Landais could get credit for capturing *Serapis*. But Landais's actions were ambiguous enough that no action could be taken against him following the battle.

Bonhomme Richard was sinking. *Serapis*'s guns had torn great holes in its opponent, and had shaken the elderly hull so that its seams were leaking below the waterline. *Alliance*'s fire exacerbated the problems. The ship started settling. Two alarmed members of *Bonhomme Richard*'s crew started shouting for quarter. Jones, enraged at the cries, shouted, "Shoot them," but threw his pistols at the pair instead of firing them. Pearson, also hearing the cries, shouted across, "Have you struck?" to which Jones is said to have replied, "I may sink, but I'm damned if I'll strike."

The final stage of the fight between *Bonhomme Richard* and *Serapis*, with the two ships lashed together. (AC)

With that exchange, the battle resumed at an even greater fury. Pearson attempted to board, but the party he led was driven off by *Bonhomme Richard*'s superior numbers. Both ships had numerous fires aboard. *Serapis*'s main mast had been shot away. *Bonhomme Richard* continued to settle in the water. Both sides could fight, but neither could win.

Around 10.00pm, *Bonhomme Richard*'s master-at-arms freed 100 British prisoners in the ship's flooding after hold. Had they taken up arms, they could have captured *Bonhomme Richard*. One or two tried. Jones and Dale, realizing the risk the released prisoners posed, set them to work on the pumps – telling them that if *Bonhomme Richard* sank everyone would drown. One prisoner jumped aboard *Serapis* and told Pearson of *Bonhomme Richard*'s state. Pearson passed the word that if his crew could last 30 minutes more, victory was theirs.

Then, suddenly, the battle shifted. William Hamilton, a seaman, had taken a slow-match and a bag of grenades on to *Bonhomme Richard*'s maintop, and had crawled out on to the mainyard. From there, he lit the fuses, and tossed the bombs on to *Serapis* where, six seconds after being lit, they exploded. Most landed on the upper works, causing minor damage. But one bounced off a hatch coaming on the upper deck and bounced on to the lower deck. During the hours of battle unused cartridges for *Serapis*'s 18-pounder cannon had accumulated on the lower gun deck, forgotten in the darkness. When Hamilton's grenade exploded, it touched off one of these charges, which set off others. Soon, between 100lb and 200lb of gunpowder went off in a chain reaction that ran the length of the lower gun deck. *Serapis*'s main battery fell silent.

With his main battery out of action, an enemy that controlled the upper works, and a fresh enemy frigate close at hand, Pearson felt that he had run out of options. By 10.30pm it was clear that the convoy had escaped, accomplishing his mission. As further slaughter was pointless, Pearson surrendered *Serapis*. Jones had won.

In a romanticized painting by Henry Pyle, John Paul Jones is shown accepting Pearson's surrender. Such a surrender ceremony did occur, although it was probably not as aesthetically staged. (MOA-UM)

STATISTICS AND ANALYSIS

While it is clear who won the battle of Flamborough Head, it is less clear as to where the advantages lay and who really held them. On paper, the Continental squadron held a clear superiority over British forces. Jones commanded six ships at the battle, together mounting 122 guns with a broadside weight of 766lb and a total of 884 officers, sailors, and Marines. Pearson had two warships, with 64 guns that had a broadside weight of 345lb, and 430 men. When the clash is approached from this perspective, the British were facing odds of greater than 2:1.

Yet raw numbers hardly tell the story. Two of Jones's six ships were small pilot schooners, prizes taken the previous day. Of his four warships, *Vengeance* was a small 12-gun brig that participated as a spectator – not even bothering to chase after the convoy's merchantmen, although there was opportunity to do so. Neither squadron fought as a unified whole. Instead the action devolved into what were essentially two single-ship actions between *Bonhomme Richard* and *Serapis* and *Pallas* and *Countess of Scarborough*.

Alliance's participation was problematic. Landais made his ship a malevolent presence throughout the battle, engaging sporadically, and firing seeming randomly into both sides. In addition to firing three broadsides into *Bonhomme Richard* and *Serapis*, *Alliance* fired at least one broadside into the battle between *Pallas* and *Countess of Scarborough*, although on that occasion it appears most of the balls went into *Countess of Scarborough*. While *Alliance*'s presence was a factor in Pearson's surrender, on balance the frigate helped Pearson more than it hurt. It did not decide the battle between the two two-deckers.

Examining the action as two single-ship duels, a different picture emerges as to relative advantage. In the battle between *Pallas* and *Countess of Scarborough*, the

Table 1. Warships present at Flamborough Head

	Guns mounted	Broadside weight (lb)	Crew present
Continental			
Bonhomme Richard	42	254	347
Alliance	36	360	215
Pallas	32	128	243
Vengeance	12	24	66
Total	122	766	871
British			
Serapis	44	285	280
Countess of Scarborough	20	60	150
Total	64	345	430

advantage lay clearly with the French frigate. *Pallas* mounted 32 guns and mustered 243 men. Its 8- and 4-pounders fired a broadside weight of 128lb. Against that *Countess of Scarborough* had 20 guns, 150 men, and a broadside of either 40lb or 60lb (records are unclear on the type of guns mounted). Additionally, *Pallas* had been built with a warship's heavier scantlings, while *Countess of Scarborough* was a converted merchantman. The wonder was not that *Pallas* won, it was that it took the frigate two hours to prevail over its weaker opponent.

In the battle between *Bonhomme Richard* and *Serapis* the advantage actually lay with the smaller *Serapis*, although Jones had the advantage in tonnage and men. His ship was over 100 tons bigger than Pearson's. Some of *Bonhomme Richard*'s crew were absent on prizes, but Jones had between 322 and 347 men at the start of the battle. Against that, Pearson had 280 men. (Morison gives *Serapis* 325 men, but this appears unlikely.)

John Paul Jones made effective use of marksmen in the fighting tops to control the upper works of both ships in his battle with *Serapis*. (AC)

But *Serapis* had a clear advantage in both speed and firepower. *Serapis*'s copper bottom and lower profile favored the British ship over *Bonhomme Richard* in the light winds in which the battle was fought. Jones wrote subsequently that *Serapis* could sail two feet to every one of *Bonhomme Richard*. With a broadside of ten 18-pounder, 11 12-pounder and one 6-pounder cannon, *Serapis* could throw 285lb of iron with each broadside. Against that – including its faulty 18-pounders – *Bonhomme Richard* had a broadside weight of 254lb. Excluding the

18-pounders – which did more damage to *Bonhomme Richard* than *Serapis* – *Bonhomme Richard* mustered a broadside of only 200lb.

Had the battle of Flamborough Head taken place a year later, the 6-pounders would have been replaced by carronades, short-barreled lightweight artillery that fired heavy shot. Establishment for a 44-gun two-decker would have given *Serapis* ten 18-pounder carronades on its quarterdeck and forecastle. With regard to the timing of the battle, the British vessel was as unfortunate with its armament as it had been fortunate with its coppering. As it was, *Serapis* had a roughly 3:2 advantage in metal over *Bonhomme Richard*.

Jones had an advantage in Marines that was greater than 3:1 – 140 Continental Marines to 45 British Marines – but that advantage came into play only when the ships were closer than 25yd apart. While the range for musket shot was 100yd, sharpshooters on the fighting tops had little chance of hitting a target on a deck when the ships were separated by more than 25yd, and could only reliably hit someone when the two ships were touching.

One of the many song sheets that circulated immediately after the battle of Flamborough Head to celebrate the action. Some songs vilified Jones. This one – *Paul Jones' Victory* – praised him. (LoC)

Each captain recognized their own strengths and weaknesses, as shown in the tactics both used during the battle. Throughout the battle Jones fired at *Serapis*'s masts and rigging, intending to reduce its mobility and allow *Bonhomme Richard* to grapple with its more agile opponent. Even at the late stages of the battle, when only a pair of quarterdeck guns laid by Jones personally were still firing, he aimed them at *Serapis*'s mainmast, to immobilize *Serapis* should the British ship break free of the grapples. He also continuously attempted to bring *Bonhomme Richard* alongside *Serapis*, and grapple in order to transform the battle into a musketry duel.

Pearson recognized the strengths that he had with *Serapis*'s superior mobility and gunnery, and used them effectively in the first part of the battle. In the first 30 minutes of combat, he effectively silenced *Bonhomme Richard*'s great guns, maneuvering to rake *Bonhomme Richard* and firing enough broadsides to put most of *Bonhomme Richard*'s upper-deck 12-pounders out of action. Had he stood off at pistol shot – 25yd – and simply poured more broadsides into the ex-Indiaman, Pearson would have silenced *Bonhomme Richard* within another hour, with *Serapis* relatively undamaged. This

A re-enactor from the United States Navy fires a Revolution-era musket. Unlike most naval battles of the American Revolution, the duel between *Bonhomme Richard* and *Serapis* was largely decided by musketry. (USN)

would have allowed Pearson either to challenge *Alliance* or to succor *Countess of Scarborough* (which was still fighting *Pallas* at that point).

Yet Pearson allowed *Bonhomme Richard* to foul *Serapis* twice over the next half-hour, and on the second try, Jones succeeded in grappling the two ships together, with ultimately fatal results for *Serapis*. It is hard to avoid concluding that Pearson had gotten a little careless, feeling that he had the battle won. Certainly against an opponent less determined than Jones, Pearson would have succeeded in taking *Bonhomme Richard* regardless, but by allowing the ex-Indiaman to foul *Serapis* Pearson ultimately conceded the battle. Even if Pearson had taken *Bonhomme Richard*, Pearson's ship would have been immobilized and damaged, and thus easy prey for the smaller, but undamaged *Alliance*.

Table 2. Casualties as a percentage of crew and crew size				
	Killed	Wounded	Uninjured	Total
Bonhomme Richard	63 (18%)	87 (25%)	197 (57%)	347
Serapis	54 (19%)	75 (27%)	151 (54%)	280

Jones made effective use of the few strengths that he had, while minimizing those of his opponent. He placed 40 men in *Bonhomme Richard*'s tops at the beginning of the battle, perhaps twice what would normally be stationed there. This superiority allowed him to clear the fighting tops of *Serapis*, and then dominate the upper works of both ships. The absence of a British presence in their tops allowed Hamilton to crawl out on to *Bonhomme Richard*'s main yard and lob grenades on to *Serapis*. A man clinging to the main yard should have presented an easy and obvious target to a marksman in the fighting tops. Pearson reduced *Bonhomme Richard* to a sinking wreck through gunfire, while Jones focused on *Serapis*'s crew to make the British vessel incapable of fighting.

The reports of casualties at the battle are difficult to assess properly. Estimates vary. The circumstances of the battle – one ship sinking and taking its muster rolls with it and the second ship, along with its muster rolls, being captured – meant that timely and accurate records of casualties were not made.

Both American and British sources accept Pearson's reckoning of 54 men killed and 75 wounded out of 280 men aboard *Serapis* as a result of the battle, although American accounts invariably point out that this was an interim count by Pearson, and casualties were likely higher. Even taking Pearson's total as a maximum, the results were bloody enough, with 46 percent of its crew becoming casualties. This was much

PAUL JONES THE PYRATE

To citizens of the United States John Paul Jones is a naval hero. For many years in Britain, he was often portrayed as a pirate. One example is the caricature right, first printed in 1779. Another early example is the song *Paul Jones, the Pirate*, a broadsheet song published in 1779, which despite the title portrayed Jones heroically. *A New Song of Paul Jones*, on the other hand, describes Jones as "Ɛ plundering Jack Paul / The greatest rogue you ever saw, man!" Rudyard Kipling wrote a poem based on Jones's exploits. Written well over a century after the battle, *The Rhyme of the Three Captains* depicts Jones as a thief, slaver, and coward.

Although some of the actions of crews under Jones were questionable – stealing the silver service from the Earl of Selkirk's manor – Jones attempted to behave as a gentleman while at sea. (He even bought the silver set back from his men and returned it.) It is hard not to conclude that the real crime that left Jones branded as a pirate by the British was his ability to beat them.

To minimize the accomplishment of John Paul Jones the British press enjoyed depicting him as a pirate. (LoC)

PAUL JONES THE PIRATE.

Pub. by A. PARK. 47. Leonard St.

One key part of the cruise of the *Bonhomme Richard* squadron was the destruction of British shipping. While some of the ships taken were sailed into port with prize crews, others were sunk or burned. (AC)

higher than the 25 percent to 33 percent casualties typically seen on the losing side of a single-ship action.

Most American sources claim *Bonhomme Richard* suffered 150 total casualties (killed and wounded) during the battle. These sources also claim *Bonhomme Richard* had only 322 men aboard during the battle, which seems understated. British sources state that *Bonhomme Richard* had 347 men aboard during the battle, with 49 killed and 67 wounded. The American estimates yield a casualty percentage of 47 percent, while British sources indicate that 33 percent of *Bonhomme Richard*'s crew became casualties.

Bonhomme Richard more probably had 347 aboard during the battle than 322, but British casualty estimates seem low, especially given the devastating rakes *Bonhomme Richard* experienced during the battle and the explosion of the 18-pounders. If we accept the American casualty figure of 150, and assume the ratio of dead to wounded remained the same as reported by British sources, then *Bonhomme Richard* had 63 killed and 87 wounded. That meant that 43 percent of its crew became casualties – a smaller percentage than that of *Serapis*, but larger in absolute numbers. Casualties on both sides were large enough that neither nation need apologize for its performance.

In the final analysis, the main reason for the Continental victory boiled down to John Paul Jones. He forced the battle to be fought on his terms. He kept his crew fighting even when they were ready to quit, and even past a point where continuing seem reasonable. He was quick to take advantage of any opportunity offered, and equally quick to turn a setback into an advantage. One example was when the freed prisoners flooded the decks of *Bonhomme Richard*. Instead of allowing them time to organize resistance, Jones convinced them to man the pumps – freeing his own men to fight while keeping the former prisoners too busy to cause trouble.

Pearson would likely have won the battle – and won it decisively – had any other French or Continental officer commanded the Continental squadron. He was an officer of above-average ability, with a record of active service. Rarely did victory in battle depend so much on one man's indomitable will, as it did at the battle of Flamborough Head.

AFTERMATH AND CONCLUSION

After the surrender, Jones sent a party to take control of *Serapis*, transferring wounded and prisoners to his new prize. He spent the rest of the night and the next day fitting *Serapis* with a jury rig so it could sail, and trying to save *Bonhomme Richard*. By Friday evening, it became apparent that this was impossible. With a storm approaching, Jones abandoned *Bonhomme Richard* at 9.00am, Saturday, September 25. It sank at 10.30am.

Jones took the remainder of his squadron with his prizes (and new command *Serapis*) to the Dutch port of Texel. He did not encounter the British warships sent belatedly in pursuit, and arrived in the neutral Netherlands on October 3, flying the Stars and Stripes. But his arrival was the start of a long period of frustration. British diplomacy forced Jones to turn *Serapis* over to France. Jones's attempts at exchanging his British prisoners for imprisoned Continental sailors were rebuffed by Britain. Payment of prize money owed his crew for the cruise kept getting delayed.

The battle made a tremendous impact throughout North America and Europe. It helped fan anti-war sentiment in Britain, where opinion was divided over the wisdom of an American war. It was a factor in the Netherlands' 1780 decision to join the American alliance. It also made Jones a celebrity – notorious in Britain and its loyal colonies, renowned in the portions of Europe and North America favoring American independence. He was excoriated by the British press and government, and exuberantly honored in France and the United States.

Louis XVI of France awarded Jones the *Ordre du Mérite Militaire* (Order of Military Merit), which made him a knight, and a presentation sword. The Continental Congress voted to allow Jones to accept the honor. It might be safe to say that Jones received everything but the two things he craved most – financial security and a seagoing command. He never received his prize money (payment was finally authorized in 1848, more than half a century after Jones's death), and, except for a brief passage back to North America, never commanded another Continental warship in combat.

His consolation prize was *America*, a ship-of-the-line under construction in New Hampshire, but the war ended before it was launched, and the ship was then turned over to France in compensation for a French ship-of-the-line wrecked entering an American port. Jones spent his remaining years seeking a new quarterdeck to command, offering his very capable services to both Russia and France.

Pearson made out better. Tried for the loss of *Serapis*, Pearson was honorably acquitted, and awarded a prized frigate command. Lionized in Britain, he too was knighted for protecting his convoy. The award prompted John Paul Jones to state, "Should I have the good fortune to fall in with him again, I will make him a lord." Upon retirement Pearson was made lieutenant-governor of the Royal Naval Hospital, Greenwich, gaining the security that evaded Jones.

The indifferent treatment meted out to Jones, in contrast to the rewards given Pearson, reflected the changing nature of the naval war. The entry of European allies reduced the necessity for the United States to maintain a navy. They could borrow one from allies when one was needed. Navies were expensive, and the United States started their war for independence impoverished, and quickly ran through such monies as they could raise or borrow. The United States had little need for naval captains, however successful, and could not afford to outfit warships even if the need arose.

French, Spanish, and Dutch entry into the American Revolutionary Wars increased the importance of the Royal Navy. England was seriously threatened by invasion for the first time in over a century, and only the Royal Navy appeared to stand between Britain and invasion. (As events turned out Spanish and French naval incompetence proved a more significant shield from invasion than the Royal Navy.) Pearson's to-the-bitter-end defense resonated with the British, especially since his efforts kept his convoy safe.

Subsequent eras have been kinder to Jones than his own times. He became an exemplar for the United States Navy from the time it was formed in 1798 to the present. It drew inspiration from his attempts to create a professional naval officer corps in the Continental Navy, but even more from his example as a fighting sailor. His goal, to always seek out and destroy the enemy, became the goal for the United States Navy as well. Only the Royal Navy and the Imperial Japanese Navy similarly embraced naval aggressiveness, rather than treating their navies as auxiliary to their armies.

With the growth of the United States Navy in the 1890s and the first decade of the 20th century, interest in Jones grew. President Theodore Roosevelt, a naval enthusiast, had a search made for Jones's Paris grave. Found in 1905, Jones was exhumed, and re-interred with great ceremony at the United States Naval Academy at Annapolis, Maryland. Midshipmen there treat the body with perhaps less reverence

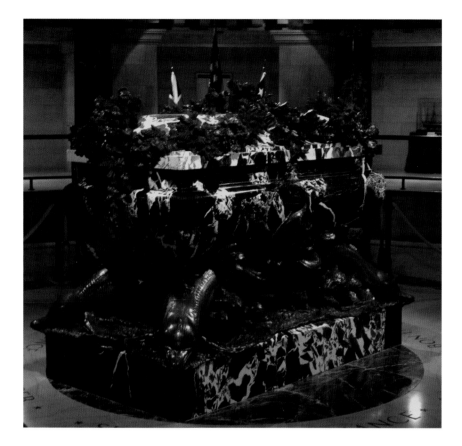

Forgotten at his death, and buried anonymously in Paris, John Paul Jones's body was found in 1905, brought back to the United States and placed in this elaborate sarcophagus at the United States Naval Academy at Annapolis. (USN)

than had been hoped when Jones was reburied. A song parody popular at the Naval Academy asserts:

> Everybody works but John Paul Jones!
> He lies around all day,
> Body pickled in alcohol
> On a permanent jag, they say.

One suspects Jones would approve the humor.

Serapis was eventually put into service by the French Navy, which employed it in a role consistent with two-deckers' usual missions, sent to the East Indies as part of a French expedition to take India away from Britain. It never got there. While anchored off Madagascar in July 1781, a sailor in its spirit room dropped a lantern in a tub of brandy, starting a fire that eventually sank the ship when it reached the ship's magazine. The wreck of *Serapis* was found in 1999, and subsequent dives have recovered artifacts.

As for *Bonhomme Richard*, it remains on the floor of the North Sea, somewhere off Flamborough Head. Despite attempts by different naval archeology expeditions at the time of writing, in 2011, the location of the ship has not yet been found. It remains the final, incomplete part of the story.

BIBLIOGRAPHY AND FURTHER READING

While there are many books about John Paul Jones, there are almost no book-length accounts of the battle of Flamborough Head. As a result, much of the information in this book comes from a variety of source, fitted together like a jigsaw puzzle. One problem is an American focus on the battle. This is unsurprising. Flamborough Head was the most important battle fought by the Continental Navy, but a sideshow for the Royal Navy. Yet good accounts exist representing both sides.

My account of the battle was my interpretation of information in four major sources – Samuel Eliot Morison's *John Paul Jones: A Sailor's Biography*, Jean Boudriot's *John Paul Jones and the Bonhomme Richard*, James Fenimore Cooper's *Lives of Distinguished American Naval Officers*, and H.W. Wilson's "Minor Operations of the Royal Navy, 1763–1792," a chapter in Volume 4 of *The Royal Navy: A History From the Earliest Times to the Present*. All are worth reading, as well as a recent biography of Jones by Evan Thomas. Other sources were consulted, including Jones's logs.

For life aboard that period's warships, it is hard to beat *The Wooden World: An Anatomy of the Georgian Navy*, by N.A.M. Rodger. As for the ships, an excellent account of *Duc de Duras* and its conversion to *Bonhomme Richard* resides within *John Paul Jones and the Bonhomme Richard*. Rif Winfield's books *British Warships in the Age of Sail 1714–1792* and *The 50-Gun Ship* provided many useful insights into the construction of British two-deckers.

A partial list of sources includes:

Barnes, John S., ed. *The Logs of Serapis – Ariel – Alliance under the Command of John Paul Jones, 1779–1780*, The De Vinne Press, New York, NY, 1911

Several expeditions have been sent to find *Bonhomme Richard*'s wreck on the bottom of the North Sea since 1976. Despite some claims, the wreck has not yet been positively identified. This is a photo of one such search, taken aboard Military Sealift Command oceanographic survey ship USNS *Henson* (T-AGS 63) in September 2010. (USN)

Boudriot, Jean, *John Paul Jones and the Bonhomme Richard*, US Naval Institute Press, Annapolis, MD, 1987

Cooper, James Fenimore, *Lives of Distinguished American Naval Officers*, Carey and Hart, Philadelphia, PA, 1846

Douglas, Howard, *A Treatise on Naval Gunnery*, 2nd edition, John Murray, London, 1829

Gilkerson, William, *The Ships of John Paul Jones*, US Naval Institute Press, Annapolis, MD, 1987

Goodwin, Peter, *Construction and Fitting of the English Man of War 1650–1850*, Conway Maritime Press Ltd, London, 1987

Harland, John, *Seamanship in the Age of Sail*, US Naval Institute Press, Annapolis, MD, 1990

Mahan, A.T., "John Paul Jones in the Revolution," *Scribner's Magazine*, Vol. 24, July–December 1898

Millar, John F., *American Ships of the Colonial and Revolutionary Periods*, W.W. Norton, New York, NY, 1978

Morison, Samuel Eliot, *John Paul Jones: A Sailor's Biography*, Little, Brown, & Company, Boston, MA, 1959

Preston, Anthony, *Navies of the American Revolution*, Prentice-Hall, Inc., Englewood Cliffs, NJ, 1975

Thomas, Evan, *John Paul Jones: Sailor, Hero, Father of the American Navy*, Simon & Schuster, New York, NY, 2003

Winfield, Rif, *The 50-Gun Ship*, Chatham Publishing, London, 1997

Winfield, Rif, *British Warships in the Age of Sail 1714–1792: Design, Construction, Careers and Fates*, Seaforth Publishing, Barnsley, 2007

INDEX